Jodie Berndt's books about how we ~~every single day, and now the gift~~ marriage is here! *Praying the Scrip~~purposeful, practical and wonderful. Make this book your go-to anniversary, shower, or wedding gift. Every married couple should have a copy!

> **Elisabeth Hasselbeck,** Emmy Award–winning broadcaster,
> *New York Times* bestselling author, wife to NFL-loving
> Tim Hasselbeck, and mom to three living children

Without a doubt, marriage is hard at times—and there are countless issues and challenges that can derail this vital relationship. Jodie Berndt understands how tough marriage can be, but she also knows that nothing is too difficult for the Lord. When we are guided by the very words of Scripture in lifting our union with our spouse before God, there's no telling how He will transform our marriage.

> **Jim Daly,** president of Focus on the Family

Marriage represents our deepest human relationship, and Jodie Berndt understands the power of prayer when it comes to establishing the intimacy and connection we crave. She makes it all very doable, no matter what your faith background looks like, how odd or cheesy it feels, or whether your spouse is willing to pray with you. As Jodie so invitingly puts it, "Do what works."

> **Rebekah Lyons,** bestselling author of *Rhythms of Renewal*

Jodie Berndt continues to create resources that will richly bless your relationships through the invitation to pray specifically in ways that are guided by Scripture. *Praying the Scriptures for Your Marriage* is a helpful, practical, and beautiful guide to prioritizing your marriage and your spouse through prayer.

> **Audrey and Jeremy Roloff,** *New York Times* bestselling
> authors and the founders of *The Marriage Journal*

Praying the Scriptures for Your Marriage is unlike any marriage book you've read. While offering plenty of rich insight and wise advice, Jodie Berndt also offers brilliant prayer guides to help you invite the power of God's transformational work and presence into your marriage. An outstanding read for any couple who wants to take their marriage to the next level.

> **Gary Thomas,** author of *Sacred Marriage*
> and *Cherish*

Having loved, read, and reread Jodie Berndt's *Praying the Scriptures for Your Children*, I was thrilled to have *Praying the Scriptures for Your Marriage* as part of my devotional routine. Jodie's words are honest, approachable, and biblical. But what sets this apart from other marriage books is its accessibility! It is easy to use but not shallow or trite. Her words will always direct you to Scripture and to the most powerful influence in your marriage—Jesus Christ.

> **Phylicia Masonheimer,** founder and
> CEO of Every Woman a Theologian

Jodie Berndt does it again! She takes the unfailing words of God and rocks us to the core with the power of prayer for marriage. When my marriage was in crisis and my prayers felt more like burdens than blessings, I needed this book. Rather than aiming our prayers at God to fix what's wrong in our marriages, Jodie encourages us to get curious with God about our frustrations and hurts through Scripture and prayer. The wit and grit that Jodie brings, partnered with the supreme wisdom of God's Word working itself out in prayer, will encourage anybody on the spectrum of time in marriage.

> **Alisa Keeton,** founder of Revelation Wellness and
> bestselling author of *The Wellness Revelation*

While we'd say we are in a happy and successful marriage, we were blown away at how *Praying the Scriptures for Your Marriage* gave us an opportunity to grow individually and as a couple. It prompted questions we needed to ask ourselves and each other so we can go even deeper with God and in our relationship together. Whether your marriage is thriving or stuck in a rut, you need to read this book! And even better, this book is more than a onetime read. Using these questions and prayers as an annual marriage "refresher" is a great plan—especially as your marriage season changes.

Alexa and Carlos PenaVega

Too many husbands and wives today are failing at their most important vocation—marriage. The research tells us that couples who pray together are not only much more likely to steer clear of divorce court but also to be happily married (most of the time). Jodie Berndt's breathtakingly honest, wise, and funny *Praying the Scriptures for Your Marriage* shows couples how to pray well for each other and how to find a spiritually grounded intimacy that sustains them amidst the challenges of contemporary life. Highly recommended to anyone wishing to forge a strong and stable marriage.

> *Brad Wilcox,* director of the National Marriage Project, University of Virginia

For years I thought, *Couldn't there just be a book to guide me through praying the Bible for my marriage?* (I'm a girl who needs tools—who needs hand-holding.) *This* book is that book. Finally, twenty-one years into marriage, I have gentle help engaging with God's Word related to my marriage in these pages and the stories therein.

> *Sara Hagerty,* author of *Adore, Unseen,* and *Every Bitter Thing Is Sweet*

Young married or seasoned couples, new believers, or mature saints—here is a dynamic new book for every marriage. We tend to forget that God's Word is called a sword in Ephesians 6:17. Every couple needs to become better at handling "the sword" for their most important relationship this side of heaven. With gentle practicality, vast experience, and deep wisdom, Jodie Berndt takes her readers on a journey of discovery and discipline, emphasizing the power and vital importance of the Word in marriage and teaching couples how to engage that power for marriage during prayer every day.

> **Matt Jacobson** (FaithfulMan.com) and
> **Lisa Jacobson** (Club31Women.com)

The *Praying the Scriptures* series includes the most transformative books I've ever read, and this book is no exception. I can't think of a better tool for marriages than praying the Scriptures for our relationships. For the couple who is thriving, for the couple who is at the end of their rope and clinging to threadbare hope, for the couple who has endured impossibly painful life circumstances . . . no matter where you are in your marriage, Jodie Berndt reminds us of words God has given us to pray—*his* words! His loving truth is the best news for ourselves, our spouses, and our marriages! Thank you, Jodie, for another life-changing book.

> **Nicole Zasowski,** marriage and family therapist and
> author of *What If It's Wonderful?*

Packed full of humor, sensible advice, relatable marriage stories, and, most importantly, biblical truth, *Praying the Scriptures for Your Marriage* is an easy-to-read and encouraging marriage resource. Jodie Berndt has done a wonderful job writing a marriage book that weaves together the realities of what couples face and the significance of what's really important, equipping readers with confidence to take their relationship to God through purposeful prayer. The insights layered in every chapter are like treasures waiting to be discovered.

> **Aaron and Jennifer Smith,** authors of *Marriage After God*

Praying the Scriptures for Your Marriage

Also by Jodie Berndt

Celebration of Miracles

Praying the Scriptures Journal

Praying the Scriptures for Your Adult Children

Praying the Scriptures for Your Children,
20th anniversary edition

Praying the Scriptures for Your Life

Praying the Scriptures for Your Teens

Praying the Scriptures for Your Adult Children Study Guide
(available at jodieberndt.com)

Praying the Scriptures for Your Children Study Guide,
20th anniversary edition (available at jodieberndt.com)

Praying the Scriptures for Your Marriage

Trusting God with Your
Most Important Relationship

JODIE BERNDT

**ZONDERVAN
BOOKS**

ZONDERVAN BOOKS

Praying the Scriptures for Your Marriage
Copyright © 2023 by Jodie Berndt

Requests for information should be addressed to:
Zondervan, *3900 Sparks Dr. SE, Grand Rapids, Michigan 49546*

Zondervan titles may be purchased in bulk for educational, business, fundraising, or sales promotional use. For information, please email SpecialMarkets@Zondervan.com.

ISBN 978-0-310-36159-6 (audio)

Library of Congress Cataloging-in-Publication Data

Names: Berndt, Jodie, author.
Title: Praying the scriptures for your marriage : trusting God with your most important relationship / Jodie Berndt.
Description: Grand Rapids : Zondervan, 2023.
Identifiers: LCCN 2022045676 (print) | LCCN 2022045677 (ebook) | ISBN 9780310361572 (trade paperback) | ISBN 9780310367093 (hardcover) | ISBN 9780310361589 (ebook)
Subjects: LCSH: Bible—Devotional literature. | Married people—Prayers and devotions. | Spouses—Prayers and devotions. | BISAC: RELIGION / Christian Living / Prayer | RELIGION / Christian Living / Women's Interests
Classification: LCC BV4596.M3 B469 2023 (print) | LCC BV4596.M3 (ebook) | DDC 248.8/44—dc23/eng/20230109
LC record available at https://lccn.loc.gov/2022045676
LC ebook record available at https://lccn.loc.gov/2022045677

Cover design: Curt Diepenhorst
Cover photo: flyzone / Getty Images
Interior design: Kait Lamphere

Printed in the United States of America

---

23 24 25 26 27 LBC 5 4 3 2 1

To
Hillary & Charlie
Annesley & Geoff
Virginia & Chris
Robbie Jr. & Mary

May the Lord make your love increase

and overflow for each other

and for everyone else,

just as ours does for you.

1 THESSALONIANS 3:12

Contents

Foreword

Jeff and I recently celebrated our ten-year anniversary. I still remember our wedding day like it was yesterday, jumping up and down when the pastor pronounced us husband and wife, rejoicing that after all the years of waiting and praying for my husband, God gave me a man who surpassed my dreams.

Then I vividly remember a month into marriage, sitting on my bathroom floor crying and thinking, *What in the world have I done?* We had gotten into a fight, and I just remember thinking, *This isn't going to work.*

I'm sure most brides can relate.

Ten years into our marriage, if I were to sit down at a coffee shop with you, I would tell you with tears running down my face that it's so much better than I ever dreamed. So much harder, and so much better. We've gone through seasons of financial stress, pregnancies, grief, raising littles, moves, new business ventures, depression, and chronic pain. Dreams fulfilled, dreams dashed—and our hearts trying to stay awake and alive in it all. We've had seasons when we've felt like two ships passing in the night, when we're running at different paces, and when I've felt very alone. We've fought hard—with each other and for our marriage.

And now as we finish this lap of ten years, our marriage is so much deeper and richer than I could have ever imagined on our wedding day. With our honest confessions, hurting hearts, prayers, pain, and dreams, we've learned that these are opportunities to know each other better, to choose to be a team, to pursue each other, to honor each other, and to open up our hearts to each other and to the Lord and learn to know ourselves better. Because the truth is, we're not the same people we were when we said, "I do," and I'm thankful for that, but that can also be scary as we change and grow.

Recently, I felt the Lord give me an invitation to tenderly love my husband like no one else has. The Lord told me he has chosen me to be the one to love him—and it truly is a gift. Jodie's book couldn't have come at a better time for us. Not only do I feel like Jodie and Robbie are counseling us with love, tenderness, and laughter, but they're also providing us with the greatest tool—praying through the Scriptures for each other. This is the best gift for any marriage because only through the Holy Spirit and God's Word and prayer can our hearts change and choose the other person, love unconditionally, forgive generously, open up our hearts to them, and entrust God with our desires and hopes. He alone is the one who changes our hearts, opens our eyes, and fills us with hope as we wait on him and seek his face. Prayer is the glue in any happy marriage.

I wanted to meet Jodie ever since I first read her book *Praying the Scriptures for Your Children*—and then read it again and again and began to keep all of her books by my bedside. She is deep and wise and has a treasure chest of Scripture hidden in her heart.

She once told me that when she's praying on her screened porch, she will sometimes reach out her hand because God's presence is so thick, she can almost feel it. That is the person I want to be thirty years from now—a woman who seeks the Lord faithfully, who has God's Word stored in her heart, and who is so full of joy and trust that it radiates out of me. Jodie is a gift to us all—a woman we can all learn from, but especially those who are a bit younger. She is the Titus 2 woman who teaches the younger women to love their husbands.

Read this book and then keep it by your bedside and pray through it regularly. It will transform your marriage and your heart.

A Note from Jeff: *I strongly encourage you guys to read through this book too! It was an immense gift to me, and here's why. I deeply desire to pray with Alyssa, but I often find myself falling asleep soon after we start (anyone with little kids will understand this) or struggling to carve out time for prayer with* *her as we go through our day. This book is ideal for praying both with her and for her. It took out all the guesswork and is incredibly practical and helpful while also serving as a compass from a married couple who has traversed these terrains before. Even if you only use one or two of the prayers at the end of each chapter, you'll be taking a major step toward connection and intimacy, one that has the power to impact your marriage both now and in the years to come.*

Thank you, Jodie, for fighting on behalf of our marriages by teaching us how to bring them to the throne room of God and giving us the greatest tool to develop a marriage that is full of love and tenderness—one that pursues a deep knowing of each other and displays the good news of Jesus to all onlookers. I pray that Jeff and I have a marriage that glorifies Jesus—to our kids and to the world—and is a legacy of a love that can only come from the Great Lover of our souls.

Alyssa and Jefferson Bethke

Do What Works

"I drop the kids off at school and I see this couple who are always holding hands. They walk along, talking and smiling like they're having some great love affair. I want a marriage like that."

I nodded, agreeing wholeheartedly with my friend. But she wasn't finished.

"Some days, though," she continued, *"I don't want to hold my husband's hand. I just want to run him over with my car."*

I laughed at my friend's honesty. And I knew just what she meant. We all long to experience a joy-filled and deeply satisfying marriage—to trust God with our most important relationship—but there can be days (whole seasons even) when experiencing that kind of marriage feels like a fairy tale. Like something in a movie, not something that could actually happen. And when my editor broached the subject of a book about praying for our marriages, I balked.

For one thing, a quick scan of my own library revealed no

fewer than twenty-eight books about marriage by Christian authors (one of which I had actually written—a lifetime ago). These books cover ways to cherish each other. To manage money together. To flirt well. To fight fair. To have better sex. To discover, as Tim Keller put it, that marriage is "glorious but hard," that it's "blood, sweat, and tears, humbling defeats and exhausting victories"—but to want to hang in there anyway.[1]

Did we really need one more volume on the bookshelf?

Not only that, but I wasn't sure Robbie and I had anything to add to the conversation. (And yes, Robbie is in this one with me. I'm writing the words, but the thoughts come from us both—and most of the really good ones are his.) He and I have been doing the "glorious but hard" thing for almost forty years and we've taught marriage courses and hosted "date nights" at our church, but we're not relationship experts. We were English majors in college; marriage-wise, the main thing our majors did was let us know not to sign our Christmas cards with "Love from the Berndt's."

And finally, we don't pray a whole lot together—at least not as much as I think we should. "I'd like to pray with you more," Robbie told me one time, "but honestly? It feels kind of . . . awkward." I knew what he meant. I tend to talk; he tends to ponder. Our prayer styles don't always mesh.

We have plenty of books, we're not marriage experts, and we don't pray as much as we could. Those are the minuses.

The plusses—the big plus—is that we do believe in the power of prayer, particularly praying the Scriptures, and it excites us to talk about how praying this way can transform relationships! God wants to do good things in our marriages, and the more we dig into the Bible, letting the words we read take hold in our hearts and animate our desires, the more our prayers will line up with his plans. We tap into a power that goes beyond anything our minds can conceive. "My word," God says, "will not return to me empty, but will accomplish what I desire and achieve the purpose for which I sent it."[2]

Robbie and I want to pray more. We want to draw closer to God. We want him to teach us to love and cherish each other in everything—from our communication to our finances to how we meet each other's physical and emotional needs. And particularly as we navigate the empty nest years, we want a marriage that doesn't grow stale but rather follows the promise outlined in the Bible: "The longer they live, the brighter they shine."[3]

> *God wants to do good things in our marriages, and the more we dig into the Bible, the more our prayers will line up with his plans.*

We know you want all this stuff too. In fact, most of the topics in this book come from social media surveys in which we asked folks what they wanted God to do in their marriage. And while not every chapter will pertain to your particular season or need, the Scripture-based prayers come with power for every relationship.

Pray as You Can, Not as You Can't

In the pages ahead, you'll read about real-life marriages—couples who've struggled and stumbled, some who are still finding their way. You'll also meet folks who are living in a sweet spot of grace. Robbie and I are sharing our personal stories, along with those from couples we've befriended and learned from over the years. And while we've changed a few names or altered some identifying details, all of the tales are true.

You'll also find a short verse to remember at the end of each chapter, along with questions for reflection. You can talk about these with your spouse (I *love* conversation starters; Robbie is less enthusiastic) or ponder them on your own. And where a chapter (or a life circumstance) reveals a need for professional Christian counseling, please pursue that. We're fans of the resources available through Focus on the Family (www.focusonthefamily.com/get-help) and from the American Association of Christian Counselors (www.AACC.net).

And finally, you'll discover a collection of Scripture-based prayers you can use to pray about every topic we cover. We love praying this way—using the actual words of the Bible to help shape our perspective—for a lot of reasons. Not only are Scripture prayers often more interesting and creative than anything we could come up with on our own, but they allow us to take Jesus up on one of his most intriguing invitations, the one where he promises that if we remain in his love and keep his commands, our joy will be full and we will live lives of purpose and impact—lives that bear fruit.

Lives that are marked by love for one another.[4]

Robbie and I have found this promise to be true over and over again. The more we delight in God's Word and allow it to shape our thoughts and desires, the more our prayers start to reflect what God is already doing. The more they dovetail with the good purposes he wants to accomplish. And the more we experience the fullness of joy that comes with transformation and growth.

To us, the "Reflect" and "Respond" sections represent the real strength of this book, as they offer an invitation to practical application and prayer. You don't have to go through the discussion prompts in any particular order (they're not meant to be formulaic or rote), and you don't have to hit every one of them. Same goes for the prayers. Pray some, all, or just one of the verses at the end of each chapter—or use the words as a jumping-off point for a longer conversation with God. Do what works for you.

Speaking of what works . . .

This is not a book about "fixing" your spouse; it is a book about bringing your cares and your questions to God— the One who works in us to give us the desire and the power to do what pleases him—and then trusting him with the outcomes.[5]

And there will be outcomes. Study after study details the benefits that come with mutual prayer—perks that include a higher satisfaction in marriage, a greater sense of emotional well-being, and even better sex. Even when you're fed up with your spouse (they left their towel on the floor, they forgot your anniversary, they were late—again), praying helps.

This is not a book about "fixing" your spouse; it is a book about bringing your cares and your questions to God and then trusting him with the outcomes.

"Prayer gives couples a chance to calm down" is how one researcher put it. "And it reinforces the idea that you're on the same team."[6]

If praying together is not something that will fly in your home—maybe your spouse isn't a believer, or they aren't sure prayer works, or one or both of you balk at what feels like an awkward or unfamiliar idea—that's okay. Pray as you can, not as you can't. And to borrow some timeless encouragement from my friend Ann Voskamp, "None of us pray alone."[7]

We may think we are praying alone—that no one sees us, no one knows us, no one understands—but Scripture tells a different story. The One who sees the whole world, time past and time future, sees us. The One who calls the stars also calls us by name, and he understands everything. And the One who knows our hearts knows God's good purposes, and he is always praying for us—praying with us—even when there are no words.

You are never praying alone.

When Robbie and I taught marriage courses at our church, we understood that a lack of prayer in a marriage in no way signaled a lack of love. One of the things we encouraged couples to do if they felt uncomfortable praying together was to consider the material, reflect on the questions, and then ask each other, "What's something I can do to support you in this area? How can I let you know you are loved?"[8]

How can I let you know you are loved?

Malachi 3:16 reads, "Those who feared the LORD talked with each other, and the LORD listened and heard." Could it be that God pays attention when we talk with each other? Might he even receive these conversations as prayers? When they're birthed in the context of marriage—a relationship designed to reflect God's covenant love and to be a picture of the gospel of grace—we have to believe he would.

From the union between Adam and Eve to the language in Solomon's song to the fact that Jesus' first miracle took place at a wedding to the Revelation promise of Christ's triumphant return to marry his people, the Bible is one big wedding story. God loves marriage.

God loves marriage—and he loves *your* marriage. Whether you're newly engaged, celebrating a golden anniversary, or somewhere in between; whether you're navigating a new transition, holding on in a really hard place, or simply longing to experience deeper intimacy and connection with your spouse; whether you're brand-new to prayer or you've been talking to God your whole life, know this:

God invites you to partner with him, through your prayers, to release his richest provision.

God wants you to come into his presence, the place where you'll find fullness of joy. And he invites you to partner with him, through your prayers, to release his richest provision.

As a bridegroom rejoices over his bride,

so will your God rejoice over you.

ISAIAH 62:5

Getting Started

*Before you marry a person, you should
first make them use a computer with slow
internet to see who they really are.*

WILL FERRELL

Our son was only seven years old, prepping for his role as a ringbearer in my brother's wedding, when he first broached the subject of marriage.

"What happens," Robbie Jr. wanted to know, "if you go to a lot of weddings and you never get picked?"

I wasn't quite sure what he was asking, so I pressed for details. "Robbie," I said slowly, "I'm not sure I know what you mean. What do you think happens at a wedding?"

"I think everyone gets dressed up and then the girl

chooses the one she wants. So what happens if you never get picked?"

I didn't know whether to laugh or cry. Having already been on a dozen different sports teams by the time he was seven, Robbie saw the whole world through the lens of athletics. To him, a wedding looked like one more opportunity to put on his helmet and compete for a starting position—and if he was already worried about not understanding the game, I realized (not for the first time) that it's never too early to start praying for your marriage partner!

If you're reading this chapter, chances are good that you've already found your teammate and, together, you've taken the field. Or maybe you got this book as an engagement present and you're itching to get out there and play. Either way, you may be asking yourself some of the questions engaged and newlywed (and even oldywed) couples ask: *How do we know if we're right for each other? Can I be sure that he [or she] is "the one"? Is it normal to have pre-wedding (or even post-wedding) doubts?*

The Myth of the Perfect Soulmate

How do you know if you've found "the one"?

That's a good question, and one that countless youth group leaders (including yours truly) have helped teens ponder. Knowing that God delights in the details of our lives,

Robbie and I have encouraged young people to think about what they want in a future spouse—to make a list of desirable attributes—and then remember God's invitation to Ahaz: "Ask anything. Be extravagant. Ask for the moon!"[1]

Today, "The List" has become a cliché in some circles ("My son prayed for a wife who had good teeth and smooth hair," one mom laughed), but the motivation behind it— to be thinking about your future spouse and praying for them—is legit. I'll never forget being with our daughter Virginia (whose own list included "someone I'd be excited to drive cross-country with—and still like at the end") when her dear friend, Cary, called with the news that she had just gotten engaged.

"Mrs. Berndt," she said, "back in high school, you told us to pray for our future husbands to be growing in Christ and to think about the particular qualities we found appealing and ask God to form them in him. So I made a list. I wanted to marry a Christian man who enjoyed church, who was out-going and extroverted (because I'm shy), who could make me laugh, who had a strong sense of duty, who was really close with his parents, who would talk kindly about me to others, and who could be open about his emotions.

"Three months into our dating relationship, I looked back at the list and realized that Evan checked *every* box. He was God's gift—and I knew I needed to take our courtship seriously!"

Maybe you have a similar story—your person is everything you hoped for, an answer to your prayers. Or maybe you have a different experience. Maybe you're engaged (or already married) and having some doubts. Is that normal?

Ethics professor Stanley Hauerwas would say so. "We never know whom we marry," he writes. "We just think we do. Or even if we first marry the right person, just give it a while and he or she will change . . . We are not the same person after we [get married].

"The primary problem," he continues, is "learning how to love and care for the stranger to whom you find yourself married."[2]

Learning to love and care for a stranger may sound extreme, but any couple who has been married for more than a minute knows that people really do change. And we may wonder, as the shifting starts to take place, if we have what it takes to enjoy a long-lasting marriage.

Robbie and I have often thought that if everyone followed the wisdom of Philippians 2—the part where Paul talks about valuing others above yourself, looking to their interests instead of your own—the world (including our marriages) would be a much happier place. We talk more about this concept in the chapter on serving one another, but at the risk of stealing our own thunder, we'll just go ahead and tell you that choosing to love selflessly—to put the other person first, to love and to cherish, for better or for worse—can be tricky.

It's tricky because not only are we always changing, but we are broken to begin with. All of us, even folks who seem to be perfectly matched, are self-centered and neurotic by nature. We are all deeply, profoundly broken by sin—and falling in love doesn't change that. In fact, bringing two independent, self-absorbed people into close (and permanent) proximity with one another can reveal flaws we might not have known we had. Comedian Eddie Cantor put it like this: "Marriage is an attempt to solve problems together which you didn't even have when you were on your own."[3]

> *Bringing two independent, self-absorbed people into close (and permanent) proximity with one another can reveal flaws we might not have known we had.*

The Good News about Marriage

We are constantly changing, we're all broken by sin, and marriage is hard. That's the bad news.

The good news is that marriage is . . . wonderful! It's ordained by God (we'll get into his grand design in the next chapter), and research points to a host of benefits that come with saying "I do," including things like greater safety and security, increased financial wealth, stronger physical and mental health, enhanced satisfaction and happiness, and even longer lives.[4]

Some of these perks will come naturally. Others will be

things we have to work at and even fight for. But there's a difference between "doing marriage" on our own—relying on our own strength, wisdom, and abilities—and doing it in the supernatural power that the Holy Spirit provides. The way we access this power and invite the Holy Spirit to work in our midst is through prayer.

Maybe you regard prayer the same way you once thought about marriage: it's new and unfamiliar to you. Maybe you find yourself hanging back, thinking you aren't worthy to approach God because of something in your past. Or maybe you just aren't sure where to begin. Just as you wonder if you've found the "right" person to marry, maybe you wonder if you're asking God for the "right" thing when you pray.

Just as you wonder if you've found the "right" person to marry, maybe you wonder if you're asking God for the "right" thing when you pray.

We get that. We spent a lot of years thinking that prayer was basically a one-way conversation in which we'd ask God for something we thought was good and wait to see if he answered. As I wrote in *Praying the Scriptures for Your Life*, I liked when prayer worked like a vending machine: request in, answer out.

But that's not how Jesus sees prayer. Just as in a marriage, Jesus wants conversation to spring from connection. "If you remain in me," he says, "and my words remain in you, ask whatever you wish, and it will be done for you."[5]

Prayer, to Jesus, is not just about getting results. Prayer signals relationship. And the more we allow God's words—the words found in Scripture—to shape our thoughts and desires, the more our requests will line up with God's plans. And the more we'll be equipped to live lives marked by purpose and joy.

So what does it look like, in practical terms, to pray the Scriptures—to use the promises and principles we find in the Bible to enhance and transform our marriages?

Here are two ideas.

1. You can take a big-picture approach and pray your way through the Bible. Download a reading plan (which can be easier than trying to plow through the whole thing from Genesis to Revelation) and, as you read, be alert to God's prompts and his promises, specific verses you can personalize for yourself or for someone you love.

When you take this approach—when you allow the Bible to become not just something you *read* but something you *pray*, using the words you read to animate your conversation with God—you discover things you might never have thought to pray for, blessings that God longs to provide. That's what happened to me with Psalm 145 when Robbie Jr. grew up and found his forever teammate.

> *When you allow the Bible to become not just something you read but something you pray, you discover things you might never have thought to pray for, blessings that God longs to provide.*

I had been praying for my son and his eventual spouse his whole life—praying, you might say, that they'd make a good team when the day came. But when Robbie's beloved Mary said yes, I began praying not just for *him* or for *her* but for *them*. And when I came upon Psalm 145 in the course of my regular Bible reading, I found a treasure trove of prayer prompts. For example:

> *Let them celebrate your abundant goodness (v. 7).*
> *Be gracious and compassionate toward them; let them*
>   *experience the riches of your love (v. 8).*
> *Equip them to trust your promises and remember that you*
>   *are faithful (v. 13).*
> *Uphold them when they fall; lift their hearts when they*
>   *are down (v. 14).*
> *Open your hand and satisfy their desires (v. 16).*

See how it works? You can turn any Bible passage into a prayer. God says he will listen whenever we pray and that his word always achieves his good purposes and accomplishes what he desires.[6]

2. You can pray topically. You can flip straight to the chapter in this book that meets a need you are currently facing. Developing better communication, handling conflict, dealing with parents and in-laws—there is no need you will face in your marriage that God has not already thought of, and provided for, in his Word.

And if you're one of those people who made a list back when you were a teenager (or if you have a grown-up catalog of desires you'd like to see fulfilled in your marriage right now), use that as a launching pad for your prayers. Ask God to bless you and your spouse with attributes and qualities that define a rich, satisfying, and lasting marriage. We'll get you started (see the prayer prompts below) with a collection of twelve verses you can use to cover everything from growing in grace to receiving forgiveness to enjoying a marriage marked by laughter and joy.

Remember ───────────────────

> May the Lord make your love increase and overflow
> for each other. (1 Thessalonians 3:12)

Reflect ─────────────────────

No matter what traits or attributes we might have put on our list (either before we were married or now), God always provides above and beyond—even when it comes to things we never knew we wanted or needed. In what positive ways has your spouse, or your marriage, surprised you? Make a new list—one that highlights the qualities you admire and appreciate about your spouse—and show it to them.

How does the idea that we are always changing challenge your views about finding the "right" person to marry? How might it equip you to better understand or appreciate your spouse over time? What role does grace play in marriage? Does this mirror your understanding of how God feels toward us?

It's never too early (or too late) to start trusting God with your marriage. Pick one or more verses from the following topic-based list and jot them on a card. Commit to praying them for your spouse, or for your relationship, in the coming weeks and watch for the ways God will answer.

Respond

Heavenly Father,

Gratitude—May our marriage be rooted and built up in Jesus. Strengthen our faith and cause us to overflow with thankfulness. (Colossians 2:6–7)

Humility—Equip us to be completely humble and gentle to each other and to our families, being patient and bearing with one another in love. (Ephesians 4:2)

Faith—May we grow in the grace and knowledge of our Lord and Savior Jesus Christ. (2 Peter 3:18)

Joy—May our mouths be filled with laughter and our tongues with songs of joy. (Psalm 126:2)

Wisdom—Give us discerning hearts to acquire knowledge and ears that are tuned to wisdom. (Proverbs 18:15)

Speech Patterns—Let us remember that the tongue has the power of life and death; may we be gracious in our speech so that our conversations bring out the best in each other. (Proverbs 18:21; Colossians 4:6 MSG)

Forgiveness—Help us admit wrongdoing so deceit cannot gain a foothold in our lives. Make us quick to confess our sins, knowing you are faithful and just and that you forgive us and cleanse us from all unrighteousness. (1 John 1:8–9 ESV)

Fidelity—May we belong only to each other, desiring each other, pleasing each other, and giving ourselves to each other in love. (Song of Songs 7:6–12)

Friendships—Give us friends who will encourage us in our marriage and build us up. (1 Thessalonians 5:11)

Honor—May we be devoted to one another in love, honoring each other above ourselves. (Romans 12:10)

Worry—Don't let us be anxious about anything. Let us present our requests to you with thanksgiving. Let your peace guard our hearts as we remember your promise to supply all our needs. (Philippians 4:6-7, 19)

Love—Make our love increase and overflow for each other and for everyone else. (1 Thessalonians 3:12)

Fulfilling Your Purpose

*Marriage is when you find that one special
person you can annoy for the rest of your life.*

"Why did you want to get married?"

When I posed that question to Robbie as we began work on this chapter, he gave me the sweetest answer. "Because I wanted to be with you all the time," he said.

"And," he added after a beat, "because I wanted sex."

Fair enough. Had Robbie asked me the same question, back when we were newly minted college grads and he surprised me with a ring, I would have said, "Because I was head over heels in love with you."

"And," I would have added, "because you asked me."

Robbie and I hadn't talked about marriage before we got engaged, and we certainly didn't head to the altar with any sort of goal or "purpose" in mind. Sure, we had big-picture ideas—I envisioned kids and the picket fence thing; I'm pretty sure Robbie wanted a dog—but we had never really considered what God thought about marriage. Or what his vision for *our* marriage might be.

Had we been paying better attention to the minister during our wedding, we might have gotten a clue:

> The bond and covenant of marriage was established by God in creation, and our Lord Jesus Christ adorned this manner of life by his presence and first miracle at a wedding in Cana of Galilee. It signifies to us the mystery of the union between Christ and his Church, and Holy Scripture commends it to be honored among all people.[1]

These words, excerpted from "The Celebration and Blessing of a Marriage" in *The Book of Common Prayer*, reveal God's two-part purpose for marriage. God establishes the marriage covenant with Adam and Eve and gives them a job: "Be fruitful and increase in number; fill the earth and subdue it."[2] Jesus reaffirms this commission with his first fruit-bearing miracle when he turns water to wine. And in Ephesians—the book in which we find the Bible's signature passage about how marriage works—Paul explains that the union between husband and wife reflects the relationship between Christ and the church.[3]

If all of this sounds like a mouthful, we might summarize God's purpose for marriage this way: Part one of our job is to bear fruit; part two is to showcase the gospel.

We'll take a closer look at how marriage mirrors the gospel throughout this book. For now, though, let's drill down on what it means to be fruitful.

Part one of our job is to bear fruit; part two is to showcase the gospel.

A Vision for Your Marriage

At face value, bearing fruit in marriage means having children. Increasing in number. Filling the earth. But that's only part of the picture. The fruitfulness charge that started in Eden runs throughout Scripture. It colors the lives of Noah and Abraham and Joseph, winds its way through the psalms, and then comes calling for every believer: "I chose you and appointed you," Jesus said, "so that you might go and bear fruit—fruit that will last."[4]

So how do we do that? How can we be sure that our lives—and more specifically, our marriages—will be meaningful and productive? What if we have different ideas about, say, the best uses of money and time? How can we merge our individual (maybe even competing) desires so we have a unified sense of calling?

These are legitimate questions—questions our friends Alyssa and Jefferson Bethke spent about three years processing as they thought and prayed about their own marriage. Knowing God intended them to be a team that was stronger together than separate, they came up with a vision statement, one rooted in the Genesis charge to be fruitful and govern the earth (including in Hawaii, where they live):

> We exist primarily to fulfill Jesus' words by living out "Your kingdom come, your will be done, on Maui as it is in heaven" in our family, our neighborhood, our relationships, our vocation, and all that we do.

To help bring this broad vision to life, the Bethkes detailed what it might look like in their family. They identified eight different areas—pillars—that mattered to them: ordering their lives around Jesus; working together as a family; gathering around the table (as a family and with guests); giving generously of time, talent, and money; cultivating and creating (anything from food to art); observing family rhythms and traditions; living with future generations in mind; and prioritizing their physical and mental health.

After spending a little more time fleshing out these pillars with descriptions of how they would play out in real life, Jeff and Alyssa transferred the whole thing onto a sign, framed it, and hung it on their living room wall. The artwork is big, captivating, and beautiful, and everyone who walks in—from the Bethkes' children to their neighbors and friends—knows in a moment what they're all about.[5]

Having a vision or purpose statement is like adding bumper guards to your relationship. It can keep you in your lane as you consider the unlimited ways to spend limited resources. And at the risk of sounding utterly unromantic, author Stephen Covey makes a good point about the purpose behind purpose statements. He says they're akin to having your own personal constitution, a standard "against which every decision concerning the most effective use of your time, your talents, and your energies can be effectively measured."[6]

Some couples write their statement in paragraph form, while others prefer bullet points that detail their core values (service, adventure, humility, and so forth). Our friends Joe and Margaret take a weekend away every year to plan and pray about their vision and purpose, and then they use notebooks to keep track of everything from their charitable giving goals to places they want to travel to the volunteer roles they'll take on at their church or in their kids' schools.

Praying about Your Purpose

Not every couple, of course, needs a formal statement. Claire and John Gilman (my mom and her husband) don't have one, other than their oft-repeated desire to bless and cherish each other, and they are some of the most impactful, fruit-bearing people we know. Mom hopped a plane—by herself—when she was *eighty* to join a team of missionaries and health-care workers in Africa. And untold *millions* of people in India have heard about Jesus in India, thanks to John's visionary work there.

Vision statements are wonderful tools, but that's all they are—tools. The power to make them work doesn't come from our own strength or striving; it comes from our attachment to Christ. "If you remain in me and I in you," Jesus said, "you will bear much fruit; apart from me you can do nothing."[7]

"Apart from me you can do nothing."

When Jesus spoke these words, he was talking with his closest companions. He knew he'd be arrested later that night, and he could have used those last few moments to talk about anything—preaching a good sermon, healing paralytics, even crafting the perfect vision statement—but he didn't.

Instead, Jesus invited the disciples to pray.

"If you remain in me," he said, "and my words remain in you, ask whatever you wish, and it will be done for you. This is to my Father's glory, that you bear much fruit, showing yourselves to be my disciples."[8]

What Jesus was saying (and what the Bethkes, Joe and Margaret, and my mom and John know) is that the way we discover our biblical calling—*the way we become fruit-bearing people who bring glory to God and thereby live out our purpose*—is through prayer. Scripture assures us that no purpose of God's can be thwarted; if we want to be people of impact, a good place to start is by asking God how he wants to work in and through us.[9]

If praying about your purpose (and doing so with your spouse) feels awkward or unfamiliar, you're not alone. Research suggests that only 4 percent of Christian couples pray together—about anything—despite evidence that points to a divorce rate of less than 1 percent among those who pray together daily (not counting saying grace before meals).[10] Even if praying with your spouse feels awkward, we encourage you to give it a try, if only for five or ten minutes. (We know couples who started by setting a timer; it's all about doing what works!)

> *If we want to be people of impact, a good place to start is by asking God how he wants to work in and through us.*

Whether you want to create a formal, long-term purpose statement based on what God reveals to you as you pray or you just want to get a sense of how he might call you to partner with him in this particular season of life, start by asking the Holy Spirit to help you answer some defining questions:

- What are your individual strengths? What unique gifts do you have as a couple? What do you find easy to do, where others might struggle?
- What do you love to do, even if it's hard? When do you feel most alive? What gives you purpose and joy?

Where do you sense God's pleasure in what you are creating or doing?

- What kind of marriage do you want to have? What do you value? What sort of message do you want your marriage to send?
- Where can you make an impact? What does your wider sphere of influence look like? What makes your "lane" unique? How might God want to use you in that space?

Those questions aren't meant to be all-inclusive; rather, they're designed to help form your thoughts as you pray. And where you come up against thorny patches—individual strengths that feel competitive, priorities that seem misaligned, personality traits or individual longings that have you and your spouse pointed in opposite directions—bring those to God too. You are his handiwork, created to do the good works he has already prepared for you to do.[11]

Your differences don't catch God by surprise; in fact, they may be the very things that equip you to fulfill your calling. They may be what makes you, as Jefferson Bethke says, "stronger together."

And that strength will be invaluable as your marriage goes through different seasons. Career changes, health concerns, geographic moves, birthing babies, shepherding teens, launching young adults, caring for aging parents—life is full of transitions, and not all of them will be easy. But when we delight in God's Word—when we allow the Scriptures to shape our meditations and desires (and *meditate* can be translated "to murmur" or "to speak about" with each other[12])—God offers a threefold, purpose-filled promise: We will continue to bear fruit. We will not wither. And we will prosper in whatever we do.[13]

Remember

> It is God who works in you to will and to act in order to fulfill his good purpose. (Philippians 2:13)

Reflect

Why did you get married? Have you ever thought about God's purpose for marriage—for *your* marriage?

God intends us to be people of impact; he wants us to bear fruit that will last. In what ways do you feel like you are flourishing as a couple? Where do you feel brittle or dry? Where have you been trying to be productive or purposeful in your own strength? When have you sensed God's power working through you?

Ask God to show you his vision for your marriage. Consider how he might want to use your particular gifts and talents for his glory. Write down your impressions and commit to praying about these things as you trust God to work in you to fulfill his kingdom purposes in and through your relationship.

Respond

Heavenly Father,

Let us live carefully and wisely, finding out what pleases you, making the most of every opportunity, and understanding your will for our marriage. (Ephesians 5:10-17)

Thank you that we are your masterpiece, created to do the work you have prepared. Give us a vision for the particular calling you have on our lives. (Ephesians 2:10 NLT)

Make us worthy of our calling. Bring to fruition our every desire for goodness. May your name be honored because of the way we live. (2 Thessalonians 1:11-12 NIV, NLT)

Fulfill your purpose for us; do not abandon the works of your hands. (Psalm 138:8 NRSV)

May we be generous (with our money, our time, and our prayers) so our lives will glow in the darkness. Show us where to go. Give us full life in the emptiest places. Make our marriage like a well-watered garden, a gurgling spring that never runs dry. (Isaiah 58:10-12 MSG)

Fulfill your plans for us. Prosper us and give us hope. Listen to us when we pray and cause us to seek you wholeheartedly. (Jeremiah 29:11-13)

May your favor rest on us; establish the work of our hands and make our efforts successful. (Psalm 90:17 NIV, NLT)

May our marriage be marked by faith, goodness, knowledge, self-control, perseverance, godliness, mutual affection, and love. Increase these attributes in our lives so that we will be effective and productive in our knowledge of Jesus. (2 Peter 1:5-9)

Equip us to live such good lives among our neighbors that, even if they talk against us, they will see our good deeds and glorify God when he comes to judge. (1 Peter 2:12)

May your grace abound in us so that in all things, at all times, having all that we need, we may abound in every good work. May we supply others' needs so that they will praise God for the obedience that accompanies our confession of the gospel of Christ. (2 Corinthians 9:8, 12-13)

You chose us and appointed us to bear fruit. Help us invest ourselves—our time, our relationships, our financial resources—in things that will last. (John 15:16)

Leaving and Cleaving

A man and his wife have a heated argument.
She calls her mom and says she is coming home.
"Oh no you're not," the mother replies. "He must
pay for his mistake. I'm coming to live with you."

Marriage involves the public act of leaving—making a lifelong commitment to your partner that takes priority even over your parental relationships. It involves being "united"' with one's partner—the Hebrew word means literally "glued" together—not just physically and biologically but emotionally, psychologically, socially and spiritually. This is the Christian context of the "one-flesh" union. The biblical doctrine of marriage is the most exciting and positive one that exists. It is also the most romantic view. It sets before us God's perfect plan.[1]

The quote on the previous page is from Nicky Gumbel's commentary on Matthew 19. Gumbel is the brains behind our favorite Bible reading plan (www.bibleinoneyear.org), which shows up in our inbox every morning. The "one flesh" thing may be God's perfect plan[2]—one that, as Gumbel notes, is exciting, positive, and romantic—but Robbie and I have yet to meet a couple who can execute that plan flawlessly. "Leaving and cleaving" (which is how the King James Version describes it) can be hard, if only because taking two separate people from two distinct backgrounds and trying to merge them into one functional and happy relationship always comes with surprises.

Taking two separate people from two distinct backgrounds and trying to merge them into one functional and happy relationship always comes with surprises.

Robbie and I got married young—fresh out of college—and the clash in our "one flesh" expectations about who was supposed to do what played itself out almost every night in the kitchen. Robbie wasn't as helpful as my dad had been, and I let him know it—sometimes with sarcasm (I billed it as "humor"), sometimes by banging a few pots and pans, and sometimes by giving my brand-new husband the silent treatment.

I also prayed. "Lord, can't you fix Robbie?" I'd say.

Meanwhile, Robbie was probably praying some "fix my spouse" prayers of his own. His mom is one of the most selfless women I've ever met, and since his dad worked so hard (often leaving their home well before daylight to get to the office), she would wake up whenever he did so she could fix a hot breakfast for him. One time, he came back from the bathroom at 2:30 a.m. to find the bed made and his wife on the way to the kitchen. "I'm sorry," she said with a laugh. "I thought we were up!"

I adore my mother-in-law. And in many ways, I want to be just like her. But that doesn't mean I'm above pretending to be still asleep when I hear Robbie stirring in the hope that he'll get up first, start the coffee, and let the dog out.

No Perfect Families

My own mother, smart gal that she is, warned me that blending two different sets of expectations, desires, and decision-making styles could be tricky. But if Robbie and I ever had a big disagreement, she said, I wasn't welcome to leave my man and come home. She said it with a smile, but I got the message: I was on Robbie's team now, for better or worse, and my first and best family loyalty lay with him.

Not every parent is as comfortable with the idea that their married children have a new team. Having "given away" all three of our daughters (as well as our son, although the wedding ceremony didn't put it that way), Robbie and I sympathize with moms and dads who find the transition bittersweet—and who, sometimes unwittingly, put undue pressure on their kids' marriages.

We also sympathize with the kids who find themselves sagging under that weight.

Tara is a young bride who wanted to take a trip alone with her husband, but her new in-laws had already booked a sprawling beach house for ten days—and family attendance was not optional. "This is their summer tradition," Tara said, "and they expect us to be with them every year."

Sharon told us how worried she was about her mother-in-law's upcoming visit. "Last time she came," Sharon said, "I hired a maid and together we cleaned the whole house top to bottom. But my mother-in-law had only been in my house for two hours when she grabbed a rag and began using it. 'I'm just getting the surface dirt' was how she put it."

Thomas struggles with his father-in-law's generosity. What looked like a blessing at first—the older man's financial help as Thomas started a business—has become a burden. "He feels the freedom to give advice, even when I don't ask for it," Thomas said. "And if I don't act on his counsel or do things the way he would, it creates tension—both with my in-laws and in our marriage."

Challenging in-law relationships are nothing new. The Bible showcases several particularly dysfunctional situations: Jacob (who woke up married to the wrong bride, thanks to her father's treachery), Tamar (who impersonated a prostitute in order to have sex with her widowed father-in-law after he did her wrong), and David (whose jealous father-in-law, King

Saul, gave his wife to another man to block David's claim to the kingship).[3] These stories must have been incredibly painful, but they didn't end there. Jacob, Tamar, and David all show up in the lineage of Jesus.[4] God took their worst pain points and redeemed them, and he can do the same thing for us.

Scripture also highlights some beautiful in-law dynamics. Ruth's steadfast loyalty to her mother-in-law transformed not just their desperate lives but, generations later, the whole world through the birth of Jesus. Peter's mother-in-law lived with him in what was evidently a domestic situation marked by mutual love, service, and delight in caring for one another. And when Moses found himself overwhelmed by the Israelites' needs and disputes, his father-in-law came up with a workable plan, which Moses gratefully put into practice.[5]

There is no perfect family, of course, and no flawless in-law relationship. But is there anything we can do to point our families in the direction of folks like Ruth, Peter, and Moses and away from the manipulative, painful, or dysfunctional patterns that may be part of our own family stories?

How to Honor Your In-Laws (and Protect Your Marriage)

"Honor your father and your mother," the Bible says, "so that you may live long and that it may go well with you."[6]

That's a command (and a promise) that doesn't expire when we get married. Nor does it come with conditions. Honoring our parents is a lifelong obligation and privilege, even when we don't feel like they deserve it.

Honoring our parents is a lifelong obligation and privilege, even when we don't feel like they deserve it.

Does that mean we must do everything our parents and in-laws want? No. It means we must treat them with love and respect—even as we prioritize and protect our own marriages. As we've looked at couples who've done the "leaving and cleaving" thing well, even amid challenging family dynamics, we've identified a handful of strategies that can help.

Don't Make Decisions without Your Spouse's Input

Parents and in-laws may have all sorts of plans or advice they want you to follow—input about everything from how you spend holidays to how you handle your finances to how you parent their grandchildren—but at the end of the day, unity with your spouse should always trump parent-pleasing. Listen to your in-laws, thank them for their opinion, and then do what you and your spouse believe to be best.

Will you sometimes disappoint your folks or even hurt their feelings? Probably. Which is why Robbie often shoulders the load when it comes to delivering news our parents don't want to hear. I'd stay awake half the night worrying that we might upset them; he can roll over, knowing we've made a good decision, and go to sleep.

Find Out What Says "I Love You" to Your Folks and Do It

Much has been made of "love languages" in marriage—affirming words, quality time, material gifts, acts of service, and physical touch—but these things apply to our parent and in-law relationships too.[7]

Is your mother-in-law big on celebrating birthdays? Plan ahead to honor her with a special gathering or, if material gifts make her feel loved, think about what she might like to receive. Is your father-in-law an NFL fan? Brush up on his favorite team and call him to talk about how they're doing—or if you live nearby, watch a game together. Send your parents a handwritten note for no reason other than to express appreciation. These little acts of kindness don't take a lot of time, but they demonstrate love and respect and help create a climate in which trust—and healthy communication—can flourish.

Trust God to Work in and through Your Marriage

Every marriage is different, but we have this in common: We're all imperfect people who come from imperfect families. We need the presence of a perfect God to work in our midst, knitting together our mismatched histories, equipping us to honor our parents and in-laws, and showing us how to establish healthy family dynamics for future generations.

God designed marriage to reflect his love for the church. He wants to restore and redeem our broken places, and in a manifestation of his limitless grace, he uses our marriages in the healing process. We know of one young husband who didn't have a relationship with his father, but his father-in-law has gently stepped into the gap. "My dad left my mom when I was five," this fellow told us, "so I never knew what a good husband and father looked like. Now I do."

> *God wants to restore and redeem our broken places, and in a manifestation of his limitless grace, he uses our marriages in the healing process.*

God glued you together in marriage. Not only that, but he is the one who holds all of creation—including our dislocated, dysfunctional families—in his hands.[8] Whatever your family background and whatever in-law pressures you face, now or in the future, you can link arms with the Lord, partnering with him through your prayers, and press forward together.

Remember

That is why a man leaves his father and mother and is united to his wife, and they become one flesh. (Genesis 2:24)

Reflect

What patterns or perspectives on marriage did you inherit from your family? What habits and attitudes do you want to repeat? What would you like to change?

How might you show love and honor to your parents or in-laws?

Leaving and cleaving means that we prioritize our spouse over our parents. Would you say you have done that effectively? If you have adult children, have you released them to be "fully glued" to their spouse? Ask God to reveal any places where you may need to establish some boundaries to allow your marriage (or your child's marriage) to flourish.

Respond

Heavenly Father,
Teach us to speak evil of no one, to avoid quarreling, to be gentle, and to show perfect courtesy toward one another and our in-laws. (Titus 3:2 ESV)

Show us how to honor our parents so that it may go well with us and we may enjoy a long life on earth. (Ephesians 6:2–3)

Work in and through our marriage—all of it, including the mismatched, painful, or broken histories we carry—to bring about good in our lives, shaping us so that we look more like Jesus, the firstborn among all the brothers and sisters in our larger Christian family. (Romans 8:28–29)

When we are frustrated with our parents or in-laws, equip us to be humble, gentle, and patient, showing our love by being tolerant with one another. (Ephesians 4:2 GNT)

May we always show family affection to one another, outdoing ourselves in showing honor to each other and to our parents and in-laws. (Romans 12:10 CSB)

When we need to have honest conversations (and risk upsetting our parents or in-laws as we work to protect our marriage), help us remember that your Spirit does not make us fearful, but that you fill us with power, love, and self-control. (2 Timothy 1:7 ESV)

Remind us that our in-laws are not our adversary. We know there is a thief who comes to steal, kill, and destroy, but you have come to give us life—life to the full. (John 10:10)

As we consider generational patterns, show us what real love looks like. Help us hate what is wrong and hold tightly to what is good. (Romans 12:9 NLT)

Equip us to do the right thing in our extended family, since neglecting to care for family members repudiates our faith. Help us live what we say we believe. (1 Timothy 5:8 MSG)

Help us leave our parents and hold fast to each other, becoming one flesh in every way. (Genesis 2:24 ESV)

Growing in Kindness

*My wife made me coffee this morning and winked
at me when she handed me the cup. I've never
been more scared of a drink in all my life.*

To outside observers, Sara and Randy have a near-perfect marriage. They are good-looking and smart, financially secure, and thoroughly committed to loving their neighbors, whether that means working in a homeless shelter, leading a Bible study, mentoring young professionals, or donating blood. If there's a need to be met—a place to show love in action—they're on it.

Which is why, when they asked us to pray for their marriage—specifically, that they'd be kinder to one another—Robbie and I were somewhat surprised. But as

Sara and Randy talked about their (sometimes negative) conversation patterns and their preoccupation with their own agendas and desires, we understood: It's easy to take those closest to us for granted, to let careless words slip, to be critical instead of affirming, or to put a spouse on hold while we give our best attention to something or someone else.

> It's easy to take those closest to us for granted, to let careless words slip, to be critical instead of affirming, or to put a spouse on hold while we give our best attention to something or someone else.

In one of his letters to the Corinthian church, Paul wrote a lot about love. You know the passage I'm talking about. You've heard it at a bazillion weddings. It's 1 Corinthians 13, and we may be tempted to gloss over these verses or even dismiss them because they've become so familiar. But when we ponder the words slowly, reflecting on what love really means, they can be transformational for our marriages.

"Love is patient," Paul writes. "Love is kind."[1] The Greek word for *patience* here is *makrothumia*, which means long-suffering. Or, even more literally, long-passioned. You know what a short-tempered person acts like, right? Picture the opposite. Picture someone who waits before expressing their anger. Someone you feel safe with. Someone who makes you feel loved.

The second half of this verse—the part where Paul says "love is kind"—is more active. It's the Greek word *chresteuomai*, which implies intentional acts of compassion and mercy, with the recognition that everyone—your neighbor, your coworker, your spouse—carries a heavy load. It's this kindness, Scripture says, that leads us to repentance and makes us want to draw close to God.[2]

Might kindness between spouses open the door to a similar heart change in our marriage relationships? Research supports this idea.

Kindness Glues Couples Together

Renowned psychologists John and Julie Gottman spent four decades studying thousands of couples to find out what makes relationships work. You might think it comes down to having good communication, no money troubles, sexual compatibility, or even supportive in-laws. These things are certainly valuable assets, but none of them is the biggie. The biggie, according to the Gottmans, is *kindness*. Kindness is what "glues couples together."[3]

Kindness, they say, is the most important predictor of satisfaction and stability in marriage. And the more someone receives love in action—an affirming word, a cup of coffee in the morning—the more they will demonstrate kindness themselves. It's what folks at the National Marriage Project call a "virtuous cycle," an upward spiral of generosity that leads to both spouses ultimately being kinder and happier in the marriage.[4]

By contrast, contempt is a killer. It's the single greatest threat to a sustainable marriage. According to the Gottmans, people who habitually criticize their spouses "miss a whopping 50 percent of positive things their partners are doing, and they see negativity when it's not there." Even a passive sort of contempt—giving a spouse the cold shoulder or responding to them with minimal engagement or interest—can lay the groundwork for a downward spiral that eventually leaves one or both spouses looking to end the relationship.

> *The more someone receives love in action—an affirming word, a cup of coffee in the morning—the more they will demonstrate kindness themselves.*

A Cure for Contempt

Robbie and I have seen this contempt dynamic in action. One fellow Robbie talked with confided that his wife explodes in anger if he ever does anything wrong—and then gives him the silent treatment, sometimes for days. We know a woman who nursed her husband through a near-fatal experience with cancer, only to have him recover and belittle her at every turn. Contempt is tearing these couples apart.

As I thought about these couples, and others, I found myself wondering, *Is kindness something you just naturally have or don't have? Are some people just wired to be kind?*

And where contempt or a critical spirit has established a foothold, is the relationship doomed?

I posed the first question to Robbie. He's much kinder than I am (I might make friends for us, but it's Robbie who keeps them), and I figured he'd have some insight.

Robbie said yes. Yes, some people are just naturally kinder than others.

And the Gottmans, as it turns out, agree. They maintain that some folks *are* naturally kinder, but that kindness can work like a muscle, getting stronger with use. It may be in short supply to begin with, but with a commitment to sustained and intentional exercise—to affirming your spouse, paying attention to their needs and desires, focusing more on appreciating their good intentions than condemning them for the bad results when things go awry—kindness can happen in all of us. It can grow.

> *Kindness can work like a muscle, getting stronger with use.*

Where there's contempt or a critical spirit at play, it helps to identify underlying issues—to figure out where the meanness comes from. In her Bible study on the book of Esther (in which a nasty fellow named Haman plots to kill all the Jews), Beth Moore writes that meanness "always identifies a threat, whether it's real or imagined."[5]

For some couples we've talked with, the problem—the threat—is rooted in jealousy. One partner resents the other's success or the time spent on a career or other commitments outside the marriage. We've seen meanness manifested as a cover-up for insecurity or even fear. It can also be an extension of a desire for control.

The problem of meanness, in other words, can be traced back to sin. Which the apostle Paul knew something about. "I know that good itself does not dwell in me," he wrote, "that is, in my sinful nature. For I have the desire to do what is good, but I cannot carry it out."[6]

I have the desire to do what is good, but I cannot carry it out.

Sara and Randy—and for that matter, Robbie and I—understand Paul's frustration. We know what is good for our marriage (we want to exercise our kindness muscle), but sometimes our best efforts fall short. We can't do it in our own strength. We blow it.

The Power to Be Kind

Thankfully, God knew—and knows—all of that. He wants his kids to be kind (especially, I imagine, when we live with each other), but he knows we need help.

Which is where the Holy Spirit comes in.

First, God meets us in our mean places. "I will give you a new heart," he says, "and put a new spirit in you; I will remove from you your heart of stone and give you a heart of flesh.

And I will put my Spirit in you and move you to follow my decrees."[7]

And then, as we give the Spirit more and more of our heart, kindness has a chance to take root and grow—along with every other manifestation of the Holy Spirit's fruit: love, joy, peace, patience, goodness, faithfulness, gentleness, and self-control.[8]

See what happens here? It's not us trying harder; it's God's Spirit motivating us, giving us both the desire and the power to do the right thing. It's not our willpower or ability (or even our "natural" kindness) that produces the change. It's supernatural.

Our friend Jeannie Cunnion writes about the Spirit's transformative work. "As we invest in our relationship with [the Holy Spirit]," she says, "and welcome Him into the intimate places of our lives where we've previously denied Him access, our lives will—they can't not—produce every kind of good fruit for the glory of God."[9]

Our lives are meant to bring glory to God. So are our marriages. They are "intimate places" where God wants to showcase his splendor. Let's welcome him in, give him full access to our hearts, and let him do what he does best.

Remember

Love is patient, love is kind. (1 Corinthians 13:4)

Reflect

Have you ever experienced the upward spiral of kindness and generosity in your marriage? Take some time to reflect on the ways your spouse has shown kindness to you. Thank them for what they've said or done.

Romans 8:26–27 says the Holy Spirit searches our hearts and helps us in our weakness. Ask God to reveal any places where contempt or criticism may have established a foothold, whether through insecurity, jealousy, fear, or anything else. Confess these things to the Lord (and if you're comfortable doing so, ask your spouse for forgiveness), knowing that God's deepest desire is to redeem and restore.

If you regularly struggle to show kindness to your spouse, consider inviting a trusted friend to pray for you and even to check in to see how you're doing. Take some time to reflect on God's kindness to you and be alert to the opportunities he gives you to demonstrate this same active love in your marriage.

Respond

Heavenly Father,
May we be kind and compassionate to one another, forgiving each other, just as in Christ you forgave us. (Ephesians 4:32)

Do not let us repay evil with evil or insult with insult (or sharp-tongued sarcasm), but prompt us to repay evil with blessing, because that's what you've called us to do so that we may inherit a blessing. (1 Peter 3:9 NIV, MSG)

In everything, may we treat each other the way we'd like to be treated. (Matthew 7:12 NET)

Keep us from using foul or abusive language. Let everything we say to each other be good and helpful, so our words will be an encouragement to each other and to our marriage. (Ephesians 4:29 NLT)

Thank you for loving us and giving us hope. Encourage our hearts as we show love to each other, and strengthen us in every good deed and word. (2 Thessalonians 2:16–17)

Don't let us get tired of doing good and showing kindness to each other, since at just the right time you promise a harvest of blessing if we don't give up. (Galatians 6:9 NLT)

Fill us with the fruit of your Holy Spirit: love, joy, peace, patience, kindness, goodness, faithfulness, gentleness, and self-control. (Galatians 5:22–23 ESV)

Let us be sure to take the plank out of our own eye before bringing up the speck in our spouse's eye. (Matthew 7:5)

Show us how to encourage each other and build each other up. (1 Thessalonians 5:11)

Protect us from judgmental or condemning attitudes toward each other; make us quick to forgive. (Luke 6:37)

Make us patient and kind. (1 Corinthians 13:4)

— five —

Talking with Love

Wife: I am not talking to you.

Husband: Okay.

Wife: Don't you want to know why?

Husband: No, I respect and trust your decision.

"Hit the ball back."

That's the advice Robbie and I gave our kids anytime we knew they'd be spending time with adults. Our advice had nothing to do with sports; it was all about being an engaging communicator. When an adult asked a question or made a comment about a particular topic, we urged our kids to return "the ball" with another comment or question to keep the point—the conversation—alive.

Some people are naturally gifted communicators. For

most of us, however, it takes some measure of effort. A willingness to ask questions. To pay attention to answers. To be vulnerable as we share information about our own interests, worries, desires, and plans. Two people can live in the same house—sleep in the same bed—but if they don't know how to talk and listen effectively, they can start to feel like they don't even know each other.

In the early phases of a relationship, it's easy—and fun—to discover things that are fresh and new and interesting about one another. Later on, the dynamics can change. Communication with your spouse may be more challenging than you thought it would be—and certainly harder than it was when you were dating.

One woman told us it was easier to share things with her sister than her husband. "She's better at helping me process my emotions," she said, "and she's known me my whole life, so I feel like she understands me."

Another wife shared how much she enjoyed talking with her coworker, who seemed to show genuine interest in the projects she was working on and who asked questions about her life. "I know my husband loves me," she said, "but he doesn't seem to care about the same things I do."

Several couples admitted to feeling like their conversations were increasingly stained by life's busyness. Robbie and I could understand that. Where we had once stayed up half the night talking to each other about everything—from our different backgrounds to our future dreams—ten years into our marriage, our conversations often became transactional: *Are you picking up the kids from soccer practice? Did you remember to call your mom back? Can you believe how much a new dishwasher costs?*

None of these scenarios—an understanding sister, a caring coworker, a busy life—represent bad things. But when we fail to give our best attention or effort to our spouse, the things we don't say can become wedges in our relationships. Left unaddressed, these gaps can grow and even create a narrative of their own: *He loves his job more than he loves me. She doesn't care how I feel. If only they understood me as well as _____ does. We just don't have anything in common anymore.*

While couples may point to a particular issue as the reason behind marital distance or tension—money troubles, challenging in-laws, the birth of children, or the transition to an empty nest—the problem is often not the issue itself but an inability or unwillingness to communicate effectively about it.

Communication involves two parts—talking and listening—and we need to be good at both. We'll talk about the importance of listening in the next chapter. For now, let's look at how we can become better talkers.

Let's Give 'Em Something to Talk About

Robbie and I once hosted a large dinner party where, to ensure a good mix of conversation at every table, we seated guests according to whether we thought of them as a Q or an L. Everything was going well—everyone seemed engaged in some lively discussion—until one of the L's noticed the scrap of paper I forgot to remove from under his plate and demanded to know what it was. Not knowing how else to handle the situation, I confessed. "You're kind of loud," I said, "so you got an L. The gal to your left is a bit quieter—she listens more than she talks—so she's a Q."

The room went silent for a beat and then erupted into laughter as the L's began identifying themselves as—and congratulating themselves for—being the life of the party. The Q's—who didn't say whether or not they appreciated the seating arrangement—exchanged knowing glances, which made them seem mysterious and alluring.

As unromantic as it might sound, good communication flourishes with a little advance planning.

Neither communication style is the "right" one; we all have room to improve. For example, I talk a lot; Robbie is a great listener (but he's not always the best at telling others—including his wife—what he's thinking). And while I'm sure there are a million little things we could do to further enhance our own give-and-take, let's look at four strategies that have proven effective so far.

1. *Set the stage.* As unromantic as it might sound, good communication flourishes with a little advance planning. Pick a regular time to connect and do your best to make it happen, even if you don't have anything major to discuss. That way, when something important does come along, the pathway to being present for each other will be comfortable and familiar. Whether it's a weekly date night or ten minutes every morning over a pot of French press coffee, establish a routine, ditch your phones, and focus on each other.

2. *Don't expect your spouse to be a mind reader.* At the risk of overgeneralizing, men and women communicate differently. We'll never forget the gal who texted her fiancé on Valentine's Day. "I can't wait to see you tonight," she said. "Also, I don't need flowers." When he replied, "Great! See you soon!" she realized he hadn't picked up on her hint. Wondering if she had been too cryptic, she forwarded the text exchange to her best friend—who immediately spotted the problem. "OMG," she replied, "he needs to read between the lines! 'I don't need flowers' means 'Flowers are the *only* thing that will make me feel special on Valentine's Day, so please don't mess this one up!'" (Fortunately

for that couple, the guy did show up with a glorious bouquet.)

Clear communication is a must. You have to say what you mean. And if you're like I am and you sometimes speak in a style that your son-in-law calls "buffering," don't blame your spouse if they miss something. Instead, add helpful cues where they're needed. In our case, once I do have a fully formed thought, I know to stop and ask Robbie, "Are you able to pay attention right now? I have something important to say."

3. *Keep it positive.* In what scientists call a "negativity bias," our brains are wired to hold on to more negative experiences than positive ones.[1] Negative thoughts stick around, and the buildup from hurtful or disparaging words can create an atmosphere of pessimism and resentment. We'll obviously need to talk about difficult things and we'll surely have disagreements, but we can choose how to frame those conversations.

You will have days—sometimes entire seasons—when finding something positive to say feels like a stretch. If that's where you are, ask God to show you your spouse in the same way God sees them. Be alert to the beauty God reveals and then speak what you see. As Proverbs 18:21 (MSG) says, "Words kill, words give life; they're either poison or fruit—you choose."

And don't forget to talk *about* your spouse, not

just *to* your spouse, in glowing terms. Speaking well of your spouse—praising them in public—actually influences you to look on them more favorably and with greater appreciation.[2] Your positive words become a gift to you both!

4. *Hit the ball back.* Robbie and I thought we invented this term for our sports-minded kids, but renowned psychologist and relationship expert John Gottman was way ahead of us. He built a "Love Lab" back in 1990, one designed to look like a romantic retreat, and watched 130 couples in action.

Throughout the day, the husbands and wives made requests for connection ("bids," Gottman says), sometimes with something as simple as, "Look at that beautiful bird!" If the spouse took the bid by showing some sign of support ("Wow! That *is* a pretty one!"), the two would connect. If there was no response—if the spouse kept watching TV or reading the paper (today we'd say "scrolling through their phone")—the bid fell flat and there was no connection.

Six years later, the results were in, and you can guess what the study revealed. Couples who largely ignored each other's bids wound up getting divorced. Those who took the bid—who responded to their partner by showing some degree of interest or support —were still married.

Every conversation, even the seemingly insignificant ones, represents an opportunity to keep the point going. Let's be alert to the bids our spouse makes. Let's hit the ball back.

Serving the Ball

I thought the tennis illustration was helpful, but when our daughter Virginia brought home a young man named Christopher (her eventual husband), I realized we had missed half the picture. Chris would walk into the kitchen and toss out a question ("How was your meeting today?") and then listen intently to the answer. All these years of parenting, and we never stressed the importance of *serving* the ball. What a miss!

"We won't discover how interesting someone is unless we make the effort to be interested in them," write Nicky and Sila Lee, authors of *The Marriage Book* and the creators of The Marriage Course.[3] Asking questions, they say, is one of the main ways "we can discover one another's opinions on everyday matters as well as how we view issues of wider significance."[4]

At face value, asking questions in marriage—*What was the best thing that happened today? Is there anything you're worried or discouraged about? What makes you feel loved?*—seems somewhat forced. Shouldn't those conversations flow naturally?

Not always.

One or both of us may struggle to verbalize what we are feeling. We may worry we'll be misunderstood, or we don't want to risk rocking the boat. Maybe we feel like we have to be strong for our partner or that the situation is just too complicated to put into words. Maybe we just aren't sure where to begin. Asking questions can help our partner identify root concerns or issues, even as we let them know they are valued and loved.

Jesus understood the power and importance of questions, and he asked far more than he answered: *Do you want to get well? Why are you so afraid? What do you think?*[5]

Jesus knew all the answers, of course. His questions weren't intended to produce information; rather, they were designed to build relationships, create conversations, and take his listeners to a new level of understanding. Which, at the end of the day, is what we all want in our marriages, right?

We all want to be deeply known.

We want to be understood.

> We all want to be deeply known.

It doesn't matter if we are a conversational L, a Q, or somewhere in between; we all want to be able to look at our spouse and ask what may well be the most powerful of all the Lord's questions—*Do you love me?*—and know that the answer is yes.[6]

Remember

Words kill, words give life;

they're either poison or fruit—you choose.

(Proverbs 18:21 MSG)

Reflect

Think about the communication patterns in your marriage. Do your words build up or tear down? Do you find it easy to confide in your spouse? Do you make time for regular, meaningful connection through conversation? Do you ask good questions?

Reflect on your different backgrounds or personalities and consider how they've shaped the way you express yourself. Ask God to reveal any areas where you may be holding back (fearing you'll be misunderstood, not wanting to rock the boat, thinking that what you have to say isn't important, and so forth), and share those concerns with your spouse.

If you don't already have a regular date night or "communication time" on your calendar, build it into your schedule. It may feel forced or awkward at first, but trust God to work in and through your conversation as you establish an atmosphere in which connection can flourish.

Respond

Heavenly Father,

Let the words of our mouths and the meditations of our hearts be pleasing in your sight. (Psalm 19:14)

Let no unwholesome talk come out of our mouths, but only what is helpful for building each other up according to our needs, that it may benefit those who listen. (Ephesians 4:29)

Words kill, words give life. Let us speak fruitful, life-giving words. (Proverbs 18:21 MSG)

Equip us to speak and listen with love, knowing that eloquent, powerful, and faith-filled words—the things we say, believe, or do—are all bankrupt without love. (1 Corinthians 13:1–3 MSG)

May we communicate with heavenly wisdom, speaking in ways that are pure, peace-loving, considerate, submissive, full of mercy and good fruit, impartial, and sincere. Let us be peace-makers in our marriage, sowing in peace and reaping a harvest of righteousness. (James 3:17–18)

May we speak no evil, avoid quarreling, be gentle, and show perfect courtesy to each other in our communication. (Titus 3:2 ESV)

When we're tempted to speak up or defend ourselves, remind us that you will fight for us; we just need to be silent. (Exodus 14:14 ESV)

Set a guard over our mouths; keep watch over our lips. (Psalm 141:3)

May our hearts be storehouses of treasure so that we will produce only good things, knowing that we will one day give an account for every idle word we speak. (Matthew 12:35–36 NLT)

Give us words that will encourage each other and build each other up, both privately and in public. (1 Thessalonians 5:11)

Let our conversations be full of grace, seasoned with salt, so we will know how to answer each other. (Colossians 4:6)

Learning to Listen

My wife yelled at me today, saying, "You weren't even listening just now, were you?" And all I could think was, "Man, that's a strange way to start a conversation."

Dinners at our house are loud, especially when the whole family gathers. I'll never forget one of the first times our son-in-law, Charlie, sat at the table with us. The conversation pinged back and forth, changing topics rapidly as people jumped in with opinions and stories, sometimes talking over one another to make a point. I thought it was all perfectly normal—it's what we had grown used to—but as I wrote in *Praying the Scriptures for Your Adult Children*, Charlie found his head spinning. "You people," he finally said, "always interrupt each other. And you always think you are right. I wanted to ask a question about something a few minutes ago, but now I don't even know what it was."

It's true. We Berndts (the women at least) do talk a lot. And some of us (okay, me) don't listen very well. Over the years, Robbie has grown used to this pattern. Once, when we were on a car trip, I decided to be purposely quiet, just in case he had something to say.

We hadn't gone more than a few miles before Robbie asked if I was okay. Did I, he wondered, need him to pull over. Was I going to be sick? (I think he thought I was dying.)

The Bible has nothing against talking—and Jesus was a wonderful storyteller—but it's clear that God wants us to know how to listen. "To answer before listening—that is folly and shame," he declares in Proverbs 18:13, highlighting the fact that listening promotes understanding.

> The Bible has nothing against talking, but it's clear that God wants us to know how to listen.

Listening is a way to show love, to let our spouse know that what they are saying is valuable and important. That *they* are valuable and important. And listening is a gift we *all* have the power to give. "Everyone," Scripture says, "should be quick to listen, slow to speak and slow to become angry."[1]

Will listening well sometimes be hard? Of course. People are not often "taught" how to listen (not like we're taught how to walk or how to read), and learning to listen may be "as difficult as learning a foreign language," writes marriage expert Gary Chapman. "But learn we must, if we want to communicate love."[2]

We can all listen—that's the good news. The bad news is that we don't always want to. Author Stephen Covey says, "Most people do not listen with the intent to understand; they listen with the intent to reply."[3] And apparently I'm not alone in my tendency to cut into a conversation. The average person pays attention for about eight seconds and can only go seventeen seconds before interrupting someone.[4] *Seventeen seconds!*

What a Bad Listener Sounds Like

As it turns out, being a serial interrupter isn't the only bad habit that can color our communication in marriage. Authors Nicky and Sila Lee identify four more patterns to avoid: reassuring, giving (unsolicited) advice, intellectualizing, and deflecting.[5]

Reassuring listeners try to help by minimizing the problem. You may want to say, "It will all be okay; you'll feel much better tomorrow" (and maybe they will), but your spouse needs to be able to express feelings of fear, worry, disappointment, or anything else without feeling like they've been dismissed.

Advice givers focus on fixing the problem. Robbie is a gifted analyst (we joke that his tombstone will read,

"Problems animated him"), but sometimes I just need him to listen before he identifies the root issue and tells me what I should do. After nearly four decades together, I'm finally learning to start some conversations with, "I know you'll have a good plan to fix this, but first I just need you to listen." And he does.

Intellectualizers try to explain the problem. If your spouse is worried or stressed, you may be eager to give them the "why": *You're not getting much sleep. I know work has been extra hard lately, and we just had that big car-repair bill. Plus, it's been rainy for the past week—I know how much you hate that.* You might be right, but sometimes being *right* is not the best way to foster a stronger *relationship.*

Finally, deflectors derail conversation through redirecting. When your spouse shares a feeling or an experience and you say, "Really? You know, that reminds me of the time . . . ," you're not being helpful. You may think you're taking their mind off a problem, but what you're really doing is communicating a lack of interest in what your spouse is trying to say.

As you look at that list, do you notice any bad habits that color your own listening style? If so, don't despair. God knew taming the tongue would be tricky—"No human being can tame the tongue," says James 3:8—but "what is impossible with man is possible with God."⁶ The Bible says that not only did God make our ears, but he's also the one who can open them.[7] And to echo Epictetus, a first-century Greek philosopher, maybe God gave us two ears and only one mouth for a reason. Maybe he wanted us to listen twice as much as we speak!

How to Listen with Love

Again, we're all perfectly capable of listening well; we just don't always choose to do so—particularly, it seems, with the people we talk to the most. We may pick up the phone if we see a friend calling but send our spouse to voicemail, knowing we'll be able to catch up with them later. And yet listening—and giving our spouse our *best* attention—is a way to live out the charge God gives us in Ephesians 5:21–23 to treat each other with love and respect.

In her book *The Flirtation Experiment*, Phylicia Masonheimer shares her struggle in this area. As a nationally bestselling author, the host of a popular podcast, and a home-schooling mom, Phylicia is always engaged in one project or another, and it's easy, she says, for her to get distracted or distant in her marriage. She thought her husband, Josh, would feel loved and respected if she thought highly of his work and said so publicly, commending him to other people, but that wasn't the case.

"I think respect," Josh told her, "looks like paying attention when I am talking, even if you have better things to do."[8]

Paying attention. It sounds so simple, and yet in our busy, distracted lives, it can be so very hard. One of our friends tried any number of ways to get her husband to focus on what she was saying before a counselor suggested a solution. "Take his face in your hands," the counselor advised, "and say, 'This. Is. Important.'"

Some husbands may find such behavior a little off-putting, but not this fellow. This guy knew he wasn't the best listener, and he was only too happy to put his face—and the good of their relationship—in his wife's hands. That simple gesture became a game changer.

Over the years, Robbie and I have found a handful of our own game-changing tools, strategies that have helped us upgrade our listening skills and show love and respect to each other. Maybe one or more of these ideas will be helpful to you.

First, we try to acknowledge each other's feelings. Communication experts teach a strategy called "reflecting back," which is just what it sounds like: Listen to what your spouse is saying, without trying to judge if they're right or wrong, and then repeat what they've said in your own words: *You must be worried about that. I didn't realize you were concerned about _____. That must really hurt.*

Acknowledging feelings isn't the same thing as agreeing with your spouse; rather, it's a way to let them know they've been heard. Reflecting back opens the door to deeper conversation.

Second, we try to listen with an ear toward identifying the main issue instead of getting distracted by things that don't matter. In business, good salespeople know how to recognize "phantom objections"—reasons people give for not buying something that don't reflect their true concerns. In marriage, the same thing can happen. We can circle an issue, voicing concerns without ever revealing and hitting the target.

I am a natural circler, and we can have conversations where I toss everything into a mixing bowl. When Robbie senses there's no real pattern to my comments or complaints, he'll often stop and ask a few clarifying questions to help determine what is really causing concern. If we don't determine the real issue, he has learned we'll keep chasing the phantoms—which will leave one or both of us frustrated and feeling misunderstood.

Third, once we feel like we've expressed our thoughts and feelings and identified the main issue, we figure out how we want to proceed. Again, here's where a few simple but thoughtful questions can help: *Is there anything you want to do about what you've just said? Is there something you'd like me to do? What, if any, action steps should we take together?*

A couple can have what feels like a rich and meaningful conversation, but if the talk doesn't lead to action (or if we keep circling the target), it won't be long before we begin to feel like our communication is pointless. We can settle into the conversational equivalent of the problem spelled out in James: "Anyone who listens to the word but does not do what it says is like someone who looks at his face in a mirror and, after looking at himself, goes away and immediately forgets what he looks like."[9]

All of these strategies—acknowledging feelings, identifying the main issue, figuring out the best action steps— can help us become better listeners, but be prepared to give grace to each other, as the process can take some time.

God promises to supply all we need, and he is always ready to hear our concerns.

And don't be shy about asking for help! God promises to supply all we need—patience, self-control, wisdom, and every other good thing—and he is always ready to hear our concerns.

"Because he bends down to listen," the psalmist says, "I will pray as long as I have breath!"[10]

Remember

Everyone should be quick to listen, slow to speak and slow to become angry. (James 1:19)

Reflect

Would your spouse say you are a good listener? Do you give them your "best" attention, or do you sometimes take them for granted or put their concerns or feelings on hold?

Take a moment to reflect on a time when you felt heard and understood. Share that experience with your spouse, along with your gratitude for the gift of their time and attention. Talk to each other about what each of you does well when it comes to listening and where you can improve as you work to show greater love and respect in your conversations.

Ask God to show you any underlying attitudes that may hinder your listening skills (pride, selfishness, jealousy, the desire to prove yourself right, and so forth). God is the one who bends down to hear you when you pray; trust him to help you listen with love.

Respond

Heavenly Father,

Tune our ears toward wisdom and our hearts to understanding, especially as we talk about _____. (Proverbs 2:2)

In our conversations, may we listen like Daniel did—showing aptitude for every kind of learning and being well informed, quick to understand, and ready to serve. (Daniel 1:4)

Show us how we can listen with greater love and respect for each other. (Ephesians 5:33)

Wise people listen and add to their learning, and discerning people get guidance. Please guide us as we discuss _____. (Proverbs 1:5)

To answer before listening is folly and shame. Help us listen first and speak later. (Proverbs 18:13)

May we listen without forcing ourselves on each other, trying to be "me first" when we talk, or flying off the handle about something our partner says. (1 Corinthians 13:3–7 MSG)

Let us know when it is time to be silent and when it is time to speak. (Ecclesiastes 3:7)

Where we have differences of opinion or understanding about _____, help us listen with humility, putting each other's need to speak above our own interests or desires. (Philippians 2:3)

Teach us to be careful and wise listeners, making the most of our conversations and seeking to understand what your will is in every situation, including _____. (Ephesians 5:15–17)

As we talk with each other, remind us to listen to you. Teach us to recognize your voice and follow you. (John 10:27)

Let us be devoted to each other in love, listening well as we honor each other above ourselves. (Romans 12:10)

Protecting Your Marriage

Husband: Honey, I don't think I can pick up the
dry cleaning on my way home. I just got in a
terrible accident. I think I broke my legs and
fractured a few ribs. Diane is taking me to
the hospital right now.

Wife: Who's Diane?

Paula and Luke seemed to have it all. Entrepreneurs at heart,
they built a thriving family business, served on the boards
of several local charities, and had the kind of home where
neighborhood kids were quick to drop in anytime, knowing Paula would make them feel welcome. When word got
out that their marriage was on the rocks and that they were

planning a trial separation, everyone—from their business associates to their closest friends—was shocked.

The real story was sobering. Years marked by a lack of regular physical intimacy and the stress of trying to balance family life with the demands of travel schedules, volunteer commitments, and work deadlines had created an emotional chasm that neither Paula nor Luke felt equipped to bridge.

To authors John Van Epp and J. P. De Gance, Paula and Luke's story is a familiar one. Many Christians, they say, are not facing a "full-blown marriage crisis," but neither are their relationships thriving. In fact, in their surveys of more than twenty thousand people, they found that "regardless of the denomination, 24 percent of married people who are active members of a church report struggling in their marriage." The real number, they say, is much higher because women were 31 percent more likely than men to report problems, and data suggests that men are less aware of relationship challenges than women.[1]

Men, in general, may be less attuned to relationship needs, but for Robbie and me, it's the opposite. Call us the exception that proves the rule, but when we did our own relationship analysis when we first began teaching about marriage, we realized I was often the clueless one. We were asked to rank how well we met each other's emotional needs on a scale of 0 to 4 (with 0 being "never" and 4 being "always"). Robbie gave me a zero.

"A zero?" I asked in disbelief.

"A zero," he said. "You don't meet my emotional needs."

I was flabbergasted. Robbie is the most levelheaded, emotionally stable man—the most emotionally stable *person* —I have ever met. I didn't think he *had* any emotional needs. And I told him so.

That was then. This is now, nearly two decades later. And now that we know about things like emotional needs— and how emotional liaisons with someone who is meeting those needs can lead to physical (and often marriage-ending) affairs—we are much quicker (well, okay, I am much quicker; Robbie has always been fast) to notice and respond to the things that can weigh on each other's heart. And even if we don't see the weak spots right now, we know we need to be intentional about strengthening our spiritual and emotional connections before the fissures appear. After all, it's easier to save a marriage by *preventing* a crisis than by trying to *recover* from one.

> It's easier to save a marriage by preventing a crisis than by trying to recover from one.

Guardrails for Your Heart

Robbie and several of his friends have a tradition where when one of their daughters gets engaged, the dads invite the groom-to-be to join them for a guys' night out. The older men offer wisdom and advice about married life and what the fellow should expect. The conversations are always punctuated by plenty of laughter, but the message and the takeaways are serious.

The men may talk about what spiritual leadership looks like in a marriage or what it means to truly cherish your wife. I've never been privy to entire conversations, but I loved Robbie's recap of the advice one of our friends gave Virginia's then-fiancé, Christopher. This friend had seen his own marriage nearly crumble after he failed to (as he put it) "pay attention" to his wife.

"Always remember," he began, "that besides God, Virginia is number one in your life. Not your job, your mom or dad, your guy friends, or even your eventual kids. It's Virginia. Listen to her. Pay attention to her. Support her.

"Virginia is number one, forever and always."

Over the years, Robbie and I have heard other couples echo the importance of supporting and prioritizing each other. Like the marriages represented in Robbie's guys' night out group, these folks have a love that is healthy and strong, but they are keenly aware of the need to protect their relationship, particularly given what God says about sin (it is "crouching at your door") and about our enemy ("the devil prowls around like a roaring lion looking for someone to devour").[2]

For example, our friends Kristin and John make sure

they are never alone with someone of the opposite sex, not even in a public place like a coffee shop. "If I have to meet a male business owner, I always ask a coworker to come with me," Kristin says. "There have been times when I've made the hour-long drive to the airport to pick up a young woman, even though it would have been much closer and easier for John to get her. It's not always the most sensible thing to do—it can be both costly and inconvenient—but we feel like safeguarding our marriage is worth the extra money and time."

Alexis and Tom share all of their passwords and have ready access to each other's phones. "It's not like we check up on each other," Tom told us, "but knowing that we might see anything at any time is a built-in guardrail.

"And," he added, "we don't get into long, private conversations with people of the opposite sex, even if they are our dearest friends. If a gal texts me, I answer her, but that's about it. We don't keep the chat going, just the two of us."

Dee and Boyd had each been married before when they met each other. "I knew what could happen when people don't share each other's interests," Dee said. "Boyd loves watching football; we have TVs in almost every room so he can keep up with the games. I'd much rather watch shows like *Say Yes to the Dress*, but when we got married, I figured I'd need to learn about football so I could enjoy watching with him. And now I do!"

I love the way Dee prioritized spending time with her husband as a way to protect their marriage, but I had to laugh when she asked if I knew that each team had "four tries" to move the ball down the field. "Four tries—*every time!*" she exclaimed. All I could think was, *I wonder how many tries a TV bride gets before she says yes to a dress?*

Catching God's Heart

Paula and Luke, the couple you met at the start of this chapter, are back together, but they would be the first to admit that rebuilding intimacy has not been easy. They wish they had devoted their time and emotional energy to protecting their marriage early on. And they wish they had known how to pray for each other.

"We both believe in the power of prayer," Paula confided, "and we were comfortable praying for other people and for needs at our church. But we never knew the intimacy that could come through praying together. We're still learning how to be vulnerable with each other, but prayer has been a huge part of our healing and reconnecting process."

Nina and Joel Schmidgall understand the intimacy Paula describes. In their book *Praying Circles around Your Marriage*, they say that one of the greatest forms of love is to call out your spouse's name to the Lord. "There is no match for the connection that is forged in prayer," they write. "It is what will catch God's heart to move in your marriage."[3]

Prayer bonds us spiritually and emotionally to God and to each other. But as we've said before, not everyone is comfortable praying with their spouse. If praying out loud together is not an option for your marriage right now, pray as you can—either silently or alone—and trust God to bring growth.

> *"There is no match for the connection that is forged in prayer. It is what will catch God's heart to move in your marriage."*

And if you're in a place where spiritual and emotional intimacy seem like a faraway dream—maybe because of sexual infidelity, a lingering mistrust after an emotional affair, or even the pain that years of indifference in a marriage can cause—you're not alone. Nor is your marriage doomed to some sort of second-class status. You can rekindle the romance you used to enjoy with your spouse—just as you can experience a passionate, vibrant life of connection with God.

Consider King David's love for Bathsheba and his heart for the Lord after the pain of adultery. Or Abraham's connection to God and the fulfillment of God's covenant promise after Abraham's early, fear-driven stumbles with Sarah. Or even our guys' night out friend, the one who counseled Chris to "pay attention" to Virginia. He and his wife both feared their marriage would never recover, but today it's one of the strongest, most mutually supportive unions we know—and they are living out 2 Peter 3:18, growing in the grace and knowledge of the Lord and bringing him glory as they share their redemption story with others.

There has never been a day when God panicked and thought, *They've ruined everything.* His heart is to redeem, restore, and renew our marriages—and to keep on renewing our love over time.

> *God's heart is to redeem, restore, and renew our marriages—and to keep on renewing our love over time.*

If we want to strengthen and protect our relationships—if we want to catch God's heart and enjoy spiritual and emotional intimacy with each other—a good starting place is confession. We can ask God to reveal the places where our hearts have been hard toward him and toward each other, and echo King David's prayer for mercy:

> *Create in us a pure heart, O God,*
>> *and renew a steadfast spirit within us.*
>
> *Do not cast us from your presence or take away your Holy Spirit.*
>
> *Restore the joy of our salvation. Rekindle our romance.*
>
> *And grant us a willingness to honor and obey you by loving and protecting the gift of our marriage.*[4]

Remember ————————————————————

> Above all else, guard your heart,
>
> > for everything you do flows from it.
>
> > > (Proverbs 4:23)

Reflect ——————————————————————

Scripture warns us not to think too highly of ourselves, but to be honest in our evaluation.[5] If you had to take the same analysis test we took, how well would you say your spouse meets your emotional needs? How well do you meet theirs? If you long to experience deeper emotional or spiritual connection, what is holding you back?

Think about the strength of your relationship. Can you identify any weak spots—maybe unconfessed sin, hard-heartedness, or pride—that, left unattended, could become fissures? What can you do to address those? Are there guardrails you need to put in place to protect your marriage?

Take a few moments to pray—either together or on your own—for your spouse. Bring their name before God and ask him to give you a greater understanding of their needs. Consider how you might show love and support in these areas, and try to identify one or two things you can do this week to build intimacy.

Respond ———————————————

Heavenly Father,

Make us alert and of sober mind so we can properly safeguard our marriage. Keep us mindful that we have an enemy, the devil who is always on the prowl, looking for ways to derail or devour us. (1 Peter 5:8)

Increase our harvest—our active goodness, kindness, and love— and make us emotionally rich so we can be generous in every way toward each other. (2 Corinthians 9:10–11 AMP, NIV)

Don't let us think more highly of ourselves than we ought, but show us how to think about ourselves and our relationship with sober judgment, measuring ourselves by the faith you give. (Romans 12:3)

You haven't given us a spirit of fear but of power and love and self-control. Show us how to love each other lavishly, without selfishness or fear of rejection. (2 Timothy 1:7 ESV)

Reveal any practices or habits we need to change to protect our marriage, and give us the humility to accept correction, since pride goes before destruction and a haughty spirit before a fall. (Proverbs 16:18)

Protect us from the trap of emotional adultery. (Matthew 5:28)

(For a husband) Help me live with _____ in an understanding way [with great gentleness and tact, and with an intelligent regard for the marriage relationship], showing her honor and respect so that my prayers will not be hindered or ineffective. (1 Peter 3:7 AMP)

(For a wife) Help me be an excellent woman [one who is spiritual, capable, intelligent, and virtuous], so that _____'s heart can trust me [with secure confidence]. May I comfort and encourage _____ and do him only good and not evil all the days of my life. (Proverbs 31:10–12 AMP)

Keep us on a path far from temptation—don't let us even go near it—lest we give our best strength to others instead of our spouse. (Proverbs 5:8–9)

May we love one another in a way that bears all things [regardless of what comes], believes all things [looking for the best in each one], hopes all things [remaining steadfast during difficult times], endures all things [without weakening]. (1 Corinthians 13:7 AMP)

Handling Conflict

*When you see a married couple walking
down the street, the one that's a few
steps ahead is the one that's mad.*
HELEN ROWLAND

Robbie and I had just moved to Atlanta. We hadn't yet made any friends, so I was thrilled when someone invited us to a party—and I was even happier when I learned that one of the party hosts played in a "dad band," so there would be music and dancing. It sounded so fun!

And it *was* fun—for the other guests. We were two hours into the party and Robbie hadn't once asked me to dance. And when I tugged him toward the dance floor, he shook me off. "We don't even *know* these people," he hissed, just loud enough to be heard over the sounds of "Livin' on a Prayer."

There I was—with a cute outfit and a handsome date and fun music and a babysitter on the clock at home—standing against the wall, watching all those fun people and feeling sure that we could be friends if only Robbie and I didn't look so boring.

After a few more unsuccessful attempts to get my husband to move (I might have even picked up his arm and twirled under it), I decided I'd had enough. I left.

Tears stung my eyes as I reached the street. I had no idea where I was—we had never been in that neighborhood before—so I just started running. And with every step, I built my case against Robbie: *Why does he have to be so selfish? He knows I love dancing; why does he have to be so self-conscious? If anybody should be embarrassed, it should be the dad who is trying to cover Bon Jovi.*

I don't know how long I was out there—long enough to get tired and start walking—but eventually I heard the hum of a car engine behind me. It was Robbie, who had been combing the streets in the dark. "Get in," he said.

I did, and we drove home with neither of us saying a word.

That wasn't the first—or the last—time our different personalities created conflict. Our kids still talk about the time Robbie refused to wear a pirate hat and an eye patch as we drove across the border to Canada. We were making a home movie (which is another story), and I thought Robbie should be "in character" for this critical scene, but he wasn't having it. "Haven't you ever heard of 9/11?" he asked as we pulled up to the booth where they check passports.

"Robbie," I scoffed, "there are four kids and two dogs in this car, and that's a *fake* pirate hat. *Nobody* will think you are a terrorist—nobody will *care!*"

As it turned out, the border guy did care, and even though Robbie never put on the hat, I got in trouble for filming their exchange.

The Joy of Conflict

Now that we're a bit older—and presumably wiser—Robbie and I agree that he was wrong to be so self-conscious about dancing in front of strangers and that I was wrong to want him to go to Canada dressed as a pirate. (So wrong!) But as we've considered our different temperaments and how they impact our behavior, we have discovered a sort of beauty in the tension, one that Charles Spurgeon would have understood. "Conflicts," he wrote, "bring experience, and experience brings that growth in grace which is not to be attained by any other means."[1]

Conflicts *do* bring experience. And grace as well, although in our experience, the growth there has come slowly. What once made me angry or impatient with Robbie has become over time the very thing that now makes me feel safe and secure. I've learned to trust his wisdom in our parenting choices, financial decisions, extended family relationships, and many other areas in which his steady, analytical nature shines as a strength.

For his part, Robbie would say that my pushing him past his comfort zone has been freeing. While he may still nix some of my "brilliant" ideas, he has learned to value my instincts and embrace things that might not add up on paper. And in what turned out to be a blessing for our three daughters at their weddings, Robbie used the experience gleaned from that ages-old party fight to grow in grace— spiritually *and* physically—and he's now an accomplished (and willing!) dance partner, even when the whole world is watching.

The Bible says we should consider it "pure joy" when we face trials, since these are the things that produce perseverance and make us mature and complete.[2] Could it be that the things you and your spouse fight about now are the very things God will use to make you perfect and whole down the road? Marriage expert John Gottman maintains that two-thirds of relationship conflict is "perpetual"—meaning, it's not going away.[3] And while we're obviously not talking about emotional abuse or physical fighting, we want to encourage

> *Could it be that the things you and your spouse fight about now are the very things God will use to make you perfect and whole down the road?*

you to see recurring conflict or tension in your marriage not as a relationship failure but as an agent of joy—a tool that, in God's hands, can increase your appreciation for each other and create intimacy.

Fight for Your Team

When Christopher proposed to our daughter Virginia, he arranged for both families to be there to celebrate. As I looked around the room at two sets of parents and four pairs of married siblings, I realized we had more than one hundred years of marital wisdom between us. What, I asked, was everyone's best piece of advice?

The group offered up plenty of pearls, from caring about your partner's interests to finding new ways to serve each other, but the takeaway I remember most came from our son-in-law Geoff, who talked about how to approach conflict in marriage.

"Remember," he said, "that you are on the same team. It's easy to forget that in the heat of the moment, but ultimately, a win against your spouse is actually a loss because if you're winning an argument, then they are losing—and that is a loss for your team. Your team is bigger and more important than any individual victory."

Approaching marriage with this mindset—that you are a team and you want each other to win—becomes even more powerful when you realize who your adversary really is. It's not your spouse. You may *think* they are the problem— they never help with the housework, they spend too much money, they always make you late, they whatever—but those issues are just spillover symptoms of our self-centered nature. The real problem—the real enemy—is Satan.

Jesus calls him the thief, the one who "comes only to steal and kill and destroy."[4]

Satan hates marriage, plain and simple, because it reflects God's love for his people. It doesn't matter how conflict-riddled your relationship is. Satan's purpose—his goal—is to completely destroy it. And when we buy the lie that our spouse is our adversary, we play right into Satan's hands.

> Satan's purpose is to completely destroy it. And when we buy the lie that our spouse is our adversary, we play right into Satan's hands.

The apostle Paul knew we'd come up against Satan's schemes. "Be careful how you live," he wrote. "Don't live like fools, but like those who are wise. Make the most of every opportunity in these evil days. Don't act thoughtlessly, but understand what the Lord wants you to do."[5]

So what does that look like, in practical terms? How do we live like those who are wise, making the most of the tension or quarrels we share? How do we set ourselves up, as Charles Spurgeon proposed, to use conflicts as catalysts for growing in grace?

Growth will look different in every marriage, but let's look at five things we can do to affirm the fact that, even though we may not yet perceive it, God is already at work.

Believe You Will Make It

When Robbie and I were newlyweds, his mom gave us some good advice. "Just because you fight," she said, "doesn't mean your marriage is bad or you're not going to make it." That was important for Robbie to hear, particularly since his parents almost never argued with each other—at least not that he saw. Had Robbie gone into marriage thinking that every union looked like his folks', we might have been doomed.

The average couple argues about 312 times per year.[6] And according to researcher Shaunti Feldhahn, how we think about conflict can make all the difference. On the one hand, if we hit a rocky patch and think we'll survive, we will do what's needed to "right the ship, patch the holes, and keep sailing." If, on the other hand, we believe things will never get better—if the ship is going to sink anyway—we may decide to stop bailing and just "work on escaping the wreck intact."[7]

Don't Go to Bed Mad

Getting angry isn't a sin; it's a normal human emotion. But holding on to that anger—letting it fester and put down roots in your heart—is a no-no. "Do not let the sun go down while you are still angry," Scripture says, "and do not give the devil a foothold."[8]

Sometimes we won't be able to resolve differences before the sun sets. Our dance party fight, for example, didn't even rev up until about 9:00 p.m. When that happens—when you find yourself fighting at night—don't keep talking, lest you say something you'll later regret. Resume the discussion when your heads are clear and you're not quite so tired. Pick a time when you can talk and then go to bed, say good night, and (if you can manage this one) add, "I still love you."

Don't Fight in Public

Don't argue in front of other people. Bring a trusted professional counselor into the mix, but don't complain about your spouse to your friends. And if your friends are people who trash their spouses (to their face or behind their back), get new friends. The writer of Proverbs might well have had married couples and their friend groups in mind when he dished up this pointed advice: "Become wise by walking with the wise; hang out with fools and watch your life fall to pieces" (Proverbs 13:20 MSG).

Be Kind

Being kind doesn't mean we can't express anger. Rather, as relationship expert Julie Gottman puts it, "Kindness informs how we choose to express the anger."[9] In other words, you don't have to throw spears at your spouse. Just put into words why you're hurt, disappointed, or angry.

It may sound impossible to be kind during a fight, but don't let contempt or aggression get the better of you. As Robbie says, "Watch what you say because you can't take it back."

Count the Cost

My mom tells the story of how irritated she was when John repeatedly left dirty dishes in the sink. She decided to pray about it. *Does he think I'm his maid?* she asked God.

In answer, God brought to her mind a video they had seen in their marriage-prep course in which the wife consistently left all the kitchen cupboards open, resulting in the husband's bumping his head. He was so mad that he decided to count how much time he spent closing cupboards, and he was shocked to realize how little time it actually took. He stopped scolding his wife and began happily closing doors in her wake, praying a blessing on her as he did so.

Inspired by this man's example, Mom decided to time herself as she loaded the dishwasher. Thirteen seconds. Thirteen seconds was all it took to clean up after her husband—and to pray. "Now," she says, "he sometimes loads the dishwasher on his own, but even if I have to do the dishes for the rest of my life, I'll cherish the chance I get to pray for him for those few extra seconds."

When You Can't Take It, God Can

It doesn't matter what you're fighting about—finances, parenting, in-laws, sex, punctuality, vacations, or anything else—use the conflict as a prayer prompt. You may think you're at your wit's end, that you've got nothing left, but that's okay. God understands. As one wife told me after a particularly bitter disagreement with her husband, "When I told God I couldn't take it anymore, he answered me gently. 'I know,' he said, 'but I can.'"

Prayer—giving our frustration and anger to God—takes the edge off. Research shows that it calms our nervous system, makes us less reactive, and shuts down the fight-or-flight response that can cause a conflict to escalate in a flash. According to a 2011 study published in the *Personality and Social Psychology Bulletin*, "Saying a prayer when you feel angry enough to lash out at someone can reduce your feelings of anger as if you hadn't been provoked at all."[10]

When we commit to bringing someone before the Lord, we begin to have a vested interest in their well-being. A warmth starts to soften our hearts.

Not only that, but when you pray for the spouse who hurts or offends you, it's hard to stay mad. When you commit to bringing someone before the Lord—asking God to bless them, protect them, and pour good things into their lives—you begin to have a vested interest in their well-being. A warmth starts to soften your heart. It may not be full-on love, at least at first, but it will grow.[11]

If you want to grow in grace and love toward your spouse (even if you don't currently like them), start with prayer.

Remember ————————————————

> You covet but you cannot get what you want, so you quarrel and fight. You do not have because you do not ask God. (James 4:2)

Reflect ————————————————

Think about the things that cause conflict in your marriage. Where do your different personalities or desires come into play? What does your partner do well when it comes to resolving your differences? What are your strengths in this area?

Ask God to reveal any underlying issues or unmet longings, places where you might need his redemptive power to bring healing or restoration. Confess any areas where your thoughts and behavior stem from selfish motives.

Remember who the real enemy is. Ask God to equip you to fight for your marriage, not against your teammate, and to show you how he might be using the hard places to help you grow in grace. Talk about any progress you see with each other.

Respond

Heavenly Father,

Don't let us repay evil with evil or insult with insult, but rather with blessing, so that our marriage will inherit a blessing. (1 Peter 3:9)

Give us the desire and the ability to love, bless, and pray for each other, even when everything in us feels hated, cursed, or mistreated. (Luke 6:27–28)

When we are insulted or suffering because of something our spouse has said or done, don't let us retaliate or seek revenge. Instead, prompt us to leave our case in your hands, knowing that you always judge fairly. (1 Peter 2:23 NLT)

Give us endurance, encouragement, and the attitude toward each other that Christ has toward us so our thoughts, our words, and our marriage will bring glory to you. (Romans 15:5–6)

Guard our minds toward our spouse; help us take captive every argumentative or pretentious thought to make it obedient to Christ. (2 Corinthians 10:5)

Teach us to treat each other as you treat us—being compassionate and gracious, slow to anger, and abounding in love and faithfulness. (Psalm 86:15)

As we consider how to respond to our spouse, remind us that a gentle answer turns away wrath, but a harsh word stirs up anger. (Proverbs 15:1)

Search our hearts; test our thoughts. Point out anything in us that offends you, and lead us along the path of everlasting life. (Psalm 139:23–24 NLT)

When we are angry with each other, keep us from sin. Help us resolve our differences quickly so we don't give the devil a foothold in our marriage. (Ephesians 4:26–27)

Equip us to live by the Spirit instead of living to gratify our sinful desires. May our marriage be filled with the fruit of the Holy Spirit, including peace, patience, kindness, gentleness, and self-control. (Galatians 5:19–23 NLT)

Give us a love that does not demand its own way. Don't let us be irritable toward one another or keep a record of wrongs. (1 Corinthians 13:5 NLT)

Help us to grow in the grace and knowledge of our Lord and Savior Jesus Christ. (2 Peter 3:18)

Experiencing Forgiveness

> *Therapist:* Your wife says you never buy her
> flowers. Is that true?
>
> *Husband:* To be honest, I never knew she sold
> flowers.

When our daughters got married, they didn't much care what the tablecloths at the reception looked like or which font I picked for the wedding program. They did, however, enjoy choosing the Bible passages to be read during the ceremony. Hillary settled on Psalm 105:1–5, a song of praise to God for the wonders he has done. Annesley chose the first part of Psalm 139, which was actually a lullaby she grew up hearing. And Virginia picked John 10:1–10, a reflection of her desire to know Jesus' voice and experience the full life that he offers.

None of the girls considered including James 3:2. No bride or groom, to our knowledge, ever has. But maybe someone should because that verse is a key piece of intel that every couple should have as they start out: *"We all stumble in many ways."*

We all stumble. Some of us lose our tempers. Some of us are chronically late. Some of us drink too much, spend too much, work too much, nag too much.

Some of us leave the toilet seat up. Every time.

> *We all stumble. Some of us lose our tempers. Some of us are chronically late. Some of us drink too much, spend too much, work too much, nag too much.*

We know, as Christians, that we are called to be patient with one another. "If you look at the Bible's teaching," writes Gary Thomas, "half of holiness centers around being patient with other people's sins, as much as it involves dealing with—or avoiding—our own sins."[1]

We also know we're supposed to forgive. When the offenses are isolated or minor, forgiveness isn't all that hard ("We do it every day," said one of our friends). But when we're confronted with an ongoing habit or pattern—with what C. S. Lewis called "the incessant provocations of daily life"[2]—forgiveness can be more challenging. And when the injury involves a significant betrayal of trust, it can seem almost impossible.

The Privilege of Forgiveness

"Will you help me? I'm dying."

Allyson closed her eyes as Wyatt's voice came through the phone. He had divorced her six years earlier, after two decades of infidelity, leaving her with nothing except a broken heart and four children to raise.

And yet here he was, calling for help. Allyson marveled at the request, but it didn't come as a total surprise. Years earlier—before the divorce—she had sensed the Holy Spirit's soft whisper. *If he gets sick, I want you to take care of him.*

At the time, the words hadn't made much sense. Wyatt wasn't sick, at least not physically, and had he been, Allyson would not have cared. She knew he had spent money on prostitutes and that his unfaithfulness had become a lifestyle—an addiction even—but, as Ruth Bell Graham once said about her marriage to evangelist Billy, she had "never considered divorce. Murder, yes, but not divorce."[3]

Allyson had been raised to believe that divorce was an unthinkable sin. The only thing she knew to do—the only thing she could do—was pray.

At first, Allyson prayed that Wyatt would come to his senses and repent of his sin. Then, after he left, she prayed that he'd get help and come home. And through it all, she prayed for her own tender heart, asking God to protect it.

"I knew a woman whose husband had cheated, and she was incredibly bitter," Allyson said. "I never wanted to turn into someone like that. So every morning, even before my feet hit the floor, I talked to God. 'Keep my heart soft,' was my daily prayer."

Allyson knew what people said about unforgiveness—that holding on to a grudge was like drinking poison and waiting for the other person to die—and she resolved to forgive Wyatt, no matter what. "Time and again," she confided, "I thought I had done so. But then God would let me know, ever so gently, that I had not.

"It was messy," she continued. "So messy. I had to deal with my anger with how badly my husband had hurt us, my fear of what the future might hold, and my feelings of guilt as I realized that in trying to be the wife people thought I should be, I had actually been Wyatt's enabler."

Now, as she heard her ex-husband's voice come over the phone, she realized he no longer had the power to hurt her. She felt free, as though the weight of unwanted chains had finally come off, and she found herself saying yes. Yes, she would help him.

That Wyatt was jobless and alone (another marriage had ended in divorce) didn't surprise Allyson. But she wasn't prepared for the signs of dementia or how emaciated Wyatt's once-large frame had become. Having drained his 401(k) to pay for cocaine and other illegal drugs, he seemed shadowlike, both in body and spirit. Allyson didn't think he had long to live. Part of her wanted to turn away, but what came out of her mouth wasn't rejection. "I'm here," she whispered.

Allyson spent the next two years helping Wyatt navigate treatment programs, hospital stays, and assisted living facilities. Sitting at his bedside one day, she heard the Lord's voice again. *This is a privilege*, he said.

Four days later, Wyatt died. Incredibly, Allyson realized it *was* a privilege to have been with him—and not just because, as he lay there, Wyatt confessed all the evils he had done and asked Allyson to forgive him. It was a privilege for her to experience, in the smallest of ways, what it must have been like for Jesus as he hung on the cross. "He was in agony," Tim Keller writes, "and he looked down on us—denying him, abandoning him, and betraying him—and in the greatest act of love in history, he *stayed*."[4]

God knows what it's like to be wronged by someone you love. Isaiah 53:3 says that Jesus was despised and rejected. Deuteronomy 6:15 reveals that the Lord knows what it's like to feel jealous and angry. And in Jeremiah 3:6–20, we see God experience the pain of repeated infidelity and, ultimately, divorce.

And through it all, he never stops pursuing us, loving us, and calling us home.[5]

> *God knows what it's like to be wronged by someone you love.*

Make Me Willing to Be Willing

The aim of this chapter is not to tell you whether or not to stick it out in your marriage. Allyson would tell you that God commands us to forgive, but reconciliation isn't always possible. There are biblical grounds for divorce—and especially if you are facing physical, sexual, or emotional abuse, we urge you to seek wise, professional Christian counsel.[6]

My aim is to help you live out Colossians 3:13, bearing with each other's faults and forgiving each other, just as the Lord forgave you. It's a tall order, to be sure, and one that demands humility (we can't think of ourselves as the "better" person; at the end of the day, we're all sinners), as well as an understanding of what forgiveness is—and what it isn't.

Forgiveness is not making excuses, tolerating an injustice, or dismissing the pain that it caused. Instead, forgiveness involves looking straight at the sin in all of its meanness and filth and choosing to extend grace. As we do that—as we refuse to allow bitterness and malice to put down roots in our heart—we discover the pathway to healing and freedom.

"When you release the wrongdoer from the wrong," wrote ethicist Lewis Smedes, "you cut a malignant tumor out of your inner life. You set a prisoner free, but you discover that the real prisoner was yourself."[7]

Robbie and I have a happy marriage, but there have been plenty of times when one of us has been wronged by the other and we don't feel ready, or willing, to forgive. The pain is still there and we want to sit for a bit in our prison and nurse it, either by giving vent to our anger or, more often, withholding affection or attention as a way of exacting a passive revenge. (Which is *not*, incidentally, an effective strategy; I'm reminded of the time our friend Lisa gave her husband the silent treatment for an entire Sunday, only to discover that he had spent the day wondering what good deed he'd done to earn a whole day's worth of uninterrupted football watching!)

One of our go-to prayers during those times when we know we're *supposed* to forgive but just don't have it in us to give grace to the other is not "Lord, make me willing"; it's "Lord, make me willing to be willing."

Make me willing to be willing to forgive.

That's a prayer God delights to answer. He can be counted on, Scripture says, to work in us, giving us "the desire and the power to do what pleases him." His Spirit helps us in our weakness, and our humility—our very inability to do anything for ourselves—acts as a magnet for his grace.[8]

The Holy Spirit equips us to forgive, but it's only part of the picture. If we want our relationship to survive, and even flourish, after a wounding—if we want to get past the hurt and be reconciled to one another and to the Lord—we don't just need to *give* mercy; we also need to *receive* it.

Here again, humility comes into play. We may know the

power of forgiveness, but deep down, we may feel like our sin is too big or too awful to truly be covered by grace.

We cover ourselves with a blanket of shame, telling ourselves we're not worthy to receive the freedom and joy that God offers—or the love that our spouse may be willing to give.

We think our offense is too big for any of that. Which, in an ironic and roundabout way, is actually a manifestation of pride.

Our sins are never bigger than God's grace, nor are they beyond his power and his desire to restore and redeem. "If we confess our sins," the Bible says, "he is faithful and just and will forgive us our sins and purify us from all unrighteousness."[9]

> *Our sins are never bigger than God's grace, nor are they beyond his power and his desire to restore and redeem.*

Confession is the way we trust the grace we say we believe in. It's the way we acknowledge that God doesn't love us because we *are* lovely; his love *makes* us lovely. And it equips us to love.

"We love," Scripture says, "because he first loved us."[10]

Remember

Be kind and compassionate to one another, forgiving each other, just as in Christ God forgave you. (Ephesians 4:32)

Reflect

How do you respond when your spouse hurts or offends you? Do you lash out in anger? Withdraw or withhold affection? Do you find yourself holding on to past wounds or reliving painful memories? If so, are you willing to be made willing to forgive?

"The reason that marriage is so painful and yet wonderful is because it is a reflection of the gospel," writes Tim Keller. "The gospel is this: We are more sinful and flawed in ourselves than we ever dared believe, yet at the very same time we are more loved and accepted in Jesus Christ than we ever dared hope."[11] Take a few moments to reflect on Keller's words. Open your heart to God's gift of grace, trusting him to care for you in your broken or hurting places. Your ability to ruin your marriage is nothing compared to God's power and desire to redeem it.

Respond

Heavenly Father,
Clothe us with mercy, kindness, humility, gentleness, and patience. Help us make allowances for each other's faults and forgive each other's offenses, just as you forgave us. (Colossians 3:12–13 NLT)

May we be completely humble, gentle, and patient, bearing with each other in love and making every effort to keep the unity of the Spirit in our marriage through the bond of peace. (Ephesians 4:2–3)

Grant me and my spouse the desire and the ability to repent so our sins will be wiped out and our marriage will enjoy the times of refreshing you long to give. (Acts 3:19)

Where reconciliation is difficult (or even impossible), help us do what we can and trust you with the outcome, remembering your command: "If it is possible, as far as it depends on you, live at peace with everyone." (Romans 12:18)

Heal our broken hearts and bind up our wounds. (Psalm 147:3)

Help us work for peace and holiness in our marriage, looking after each other so we won't fail to receive the grace of God. Keep us watchful so that no poisonous root of bitterness grows up to cause trouble in our marriage. (Hebrews 12:14–15 NLT)

Thank you for the gift of the Holy Spirit, who helps us in our weakness when we don't have the strength or the desire to forgive and who intercedes on our behalf. Work in all things in our marriage to bring about good. (Romans 8:26–28)

Don't let us repay evil with evil or insult with insult—no retaliation or sharp-tongued sarcasm. Instead, let us repay evil with blessing so that we will be a blessing to each other and get a blessing. (1 Peter 3:9 NIV, MSG)

Give us the strength and the desire to confess our sins to each other and pray for each other so that our marriage can be healed. (James 5:16)

When we are insulted or wounded, may we respond as Jesus did, not by retaliating or making threats but by entrusting ourselves to you, the one who judges justly. (1 Peter 2:23)

Create in us clean hearts, O God. Renew a loyal spirit in our marriage. Do not banish us from your presence or take away your Holy Spirit. Restore to us the joy of our salvation, and make us willing to obey you. (Psalm 51:10–12 NLT)

Remind us that there is no condemnation for those who are in Christ Jesus and that neither height nor depth, nor anything else in all creation, will be able to separate us from the love of God that is in Christ Jesus our Lord. (Romans 8:1, 39)

CHAPTER

— ten —

Enjoying Good Sex

My wife just found out I replaced our bed
with a trampoline. She hit the roof.

In a 2001 episode of the hit sitcom *Everybody Loves Raymond*, Debra, Ray's wife, walks in and says she's "exhausted." Figuring that means no sex for him, Ray accuses her of putting on an "I'm tired" show—a "preemptive strike," as he calls it. Debra is not happy.

The next day Ray comes home with a peace offering—an adult board game that he hopes will ignite Debra's amorous interests. The plan backfires when Ray realizes that the game includes "romantic" squares (*Write each other a poem*) and "naughty" squares (*Remove an article of your partner's clothing without using your hands*)—and he only wants the naughty ones.[1]

The interplay gets a lot of laughs. Viewers can relate to the differences in sexual desire. In fact, this variation is one of the most common problems married couples face in their sex lives. And it's not just a handful of couples who cite issues with physical intimacy. One survey revealed that almost 80 percent of married couples say they are dealing with some form of sexual struggle in their marriage.[2]

Of the *Everybody Loves Raymond* episode, one reviewer noted that it wasn't "conventionally funny," but that it did get "couples talking about their sex lives."[3]

Which is more, unfortunately, than we can say of the church. We don't, as a Christian culture, talk a lot about the joy of sex within marriage. "We spend so much time teaching people to save sex for marriage," writes counselor Debra Fileta, "but so little time teaching them to savor it after marriage."[4]

And God's plan *is* for savoring! He loves married sex—and he wants us to enjoy it. The Bible tells husbands to rejoice in their wives, to delight in their breasts, and to be intoxicated with love. It celebrates a woman who initiates lovemaking, calling her lover to join her for a vineyard rendezvous. And it even goes so far as to warn married couples against *not* having sex, except for a limited time, in order to keep us from being tempted to sin because we lack self-control.[5]

> Sex—the ability to express love through the physical union of husband and wife—is a gift from the One who is love.

Sex—the ability to express love through the physical union of husband and wife—is a gift from the One who is love. So why aren't we enjoying it more?

Why We Don't Have More Sex

Our views about sex take shape long before we get married—and our perspective is often distorted. The entertainment industry is partly to blame. Hollywood's depiction of sex is almost always between attractive people who don't need to brush their teeth and who are—gah—rarely married (at least not to each other). That can create unrealistic "sexpectations" and sow seeds of worry and self-doubt. *Am I thin enough? Muscular enough? Good enough at lovemaking? How's my hair?*

Then, too, there may be painful consequences from past encounters or from the trauma of sexual abuse. One or both spouses may struggle with feelings of deep guilt or shame.

Even those who've kept themselves "pure," waiting until marriage to experience sex, may find themselves facing mental and emotional hurdles. "How," one young bride asked, "am I supposed to move from all these years of resisting my sexual desires as a single person to suddenly letting it go—to being a sexy, secure, and passionate lover—when I get married? Am I just supposed to flip a switch?"

Robbie and I don't pretend to have all the answers, and if physical intimacy is a pain point in your marriage (especially if there's a history of abuse, pornography use, or same-sex attraction), we cannot overstate the value of professional help from a licensed Christian counselor. A lack of a fulfilling sex life—or a lack of *any* sex life—can signal that something else, something deeper, is broken. Once that problem is identified and addressed, physical intimacy can improve.[6]

Again, we don't have all the answers. But having talked with more than one hundred couples who've struggled with physical intimacy in their marriages, we can point to at least three common intimacy blockers: fatigue, stress, and differences in desire.

Fatigue

Debra Romano may be a fictitious wife, but the exhaustion factor is real. Toddlers who don't sleep through the night, teens who keep you awake until they get home, careers that sap time and energy, aging parents who need extra help—if you're not tired today, you will be tomorrow. For many women (and plenty of men), the idea of "going to bed" means just one thing. And it isn't sex.

Francie Winslow, a self-described "intimacy evangelist" and host of the *Heaven in Your Home* podcast, understands the weariness factor. She and her husband have six children, and the best way she has found to make the transition from "tired mom" to "ready wife" is to go into her bathroom, shut the door, and take time for herself.

"Sometimes I take a shower, sometimes I put on perfume or nice lingerie—whatever makes me feel pretty and fresh," she says, "and then I deliberately choose to anticipate pleasure. I thank God for my body. I remember that sex is a gift—that physical intimacy can make room for spiritual intimacy—and I choose connection."

As a fellow tired mom, I love Francie's game plan. And I'd perhaps add that the four sexiest words a man can say to his wife just might be, "I'll do the dishes."

Stress

The reason for an underwhelming sex life can often be traced to an overwhelming schedule. The busyness of our lives—family commitments, career demands, ministry opportunities, and even things that are supposed to relieve stress (like workouts and date nights)—can fill up every last white space on the calendar. Without realizing it, we can become like the ancient Romans—people "so absorbed in their 'God projects' that they didn't notice God right in front of them, like a huge rock in the middle of the road. And so they stumbled into him and went sprawling."[7]

God never intended for us to live overwhelmed lives; his desire is for us to experience his peace. To do this, we may need to reorder our priorities so they line up with God's plans. And wouldn't you know it, one of God's stress-reducing plans is for us to have sex! The chemicals released during sex actually work to fight off negative emotions and provide significant physiological benefits, including "decreased stress levels, increased oxytocin (the bonding chemical), decreased blood pressure, and an increased sense of intimacy between you and your spouse."[8]

Take a hard look at your schedule. Eliminate activities and commitments, figure out what you need to do to relax, and then—you guessed it—put regular lovemaking into the mix. Scheduling sex may sound unromantic, but it actually allows anticipation to build. And for those who, ahem, don't always welcome a sudden advance while we're cooking dinner and calling out words for the next day's spelling test, it provides the comforting reassurance that intimacy will happen right on time.

> *Eliminate activities and commitments, figure out what you need to do to relax, and then put regular lovemaking into the mix.*

Differences in Desire

Much has been made about the disparity between a man's sex drive and a woman's. Study after study (and joke after joke) points to the fact that men think about sex and want sex about a bazillion times more than women do. There are obviously exceptions—I can think of at least two in my immediate circle of friends—but rather than quibble over how much or how often, let's talk about what needs to happen to get us all in the mood.

Men and women both value affirmation ("I love the feeling of being held in your strong arms," "I'm so attracted to your _____"). And healthy communication about sex—what we like, what we don't like—is a lovemaking must. Beyond these things, though—beyond our shared desire for affirmation and our mutual need to speak up—we may well have different needs.

Experts say that what a man wants even more than his wife's *willingness* is her *desire*. He loves it not just when she responds to him, but when she *initiates* lovemaking.[9]

Women are a bit more complex. If a man wants to have sex, he's advised to remember one thing: "*Foreplay starts in the morning.* Every glance, every conversation, every act of service (or lack thereof), is either building emotional connection, and therefore fueling sexual attraction, or hindering it."[10]

The Best Sex

Fatigue, stress, and mismatched desires are only part of the picture. We're also dealing with a field that keeps flipping. Children, illness, career changes, and age all bring changes to our marriages—and consequently to our sex lives. We need to acknowledge and adapt to these changes if we want physical intimacy to continue to flourish and grow over time.

After nearly four decades of marriage, including seasons when childbirth, illness, or work travel kept us apart, Robbie and I would say that the best sex hasn't come when I've initiated, when he's helped with the housework, or even when the kids grew up and moved out of the house (although all of those things have been major plusses in terms of sparking romance). The best sex has happened—and continues to happen—as we give ourselves to each other, submitting to each other's needs and desires, secure in the knowledge that we belong exclusively to each other.

We need to acknowledge and adapt to changes if we want physical intimacy to continue to flourish and grow over time.

The Bible says we are each other's covenant partner.[11] And just as God called people like Moses and Nehemiah to renew their covenants—to gather the Israelites to remember and recommit to following God—so we need to remember our call and recommit to each other, regardless of the fatigue, stress, or changing circumstances that color our lives. Sex does that. Sex is our covenant renewal ceremony.

The best sex isn't getting; it's giving. It's coming before one another as Adam and Eve did in the garden, naked and without shame, knowing we belong only to each other.[12] And every time we come together, no matter how long or how short we've been married, we reaffirm that most beautiful wedding vow: "With all that I am and all that I have, I honor you."

Remember ————————————————

> Adam and his wife were both naked, and they felt
> no shame. (Genesis 2:25)

Reflect ————————————————

God's plan for marriage is one of mutual respecting, honoring, and cherishing—"a love marked by giving, not getting" (Ephesians 5:21–25 MSG). In what ways is your sex life fulfilling that charge? What does your spouse do that makes you feel cherished? What might you do—show more restraint or take the initiative, for example—to honor your spouse?

Talking about sex can be awkward, but communication is key. Make time (plan ahead) for a conversation with your spouse. Think of three affirmations and share these with each other, ask candid questions, and identify at least one area where you want intimacy to grow or change.

God wants us to enjoy physical intimacy in marriage without any shame. Don't be shy about inviting him into the conversation as you talk and pray with your spouse. Bring God your questions and concerns, knowing that his deepest desire is to restore and redeem broken places and equip us to give all that we have and all that we are to each other.

Respond

Heavenly Father,

(For a wife) May I be a fountain of blessing for my husband, satisfying him and intoxicating him with my love. (Proverbs 5:18–19)

(For a husband) May I enjoy the wife I married—lovely as an angel, beautiful as a rose—and never quit taking delight in her body. (Proverbs 5:18–19 MSG)

Give us a balanced and fulfilling sexual life in a world of sexual disorder. Make our marriage bed a place of mutuality—one where we seek to satisfy each other. Help us remember that marriage is not a place to "stand up for your rights"; rather, it is a "decision to serve the other, whether in bed or out." (1 Corinthians 7:3–4 MSG)

Do not let us deprive each other sexually—except when we agree, for a time, to devote ourselves to prayer. Then bring us together again so Satan will not tempt us because of our lack of self-control. (1 Corinthians 7:5 CSB)

When I feel unattractive or undesirable, or when I struggle with body image issues, remind me of the truth: You created me. I am fearfully and wonderfully made; your works are wonderful! (Psalm 139:13–14)

Bless our union—physically, but also emotionally, socially, and spiritually; make our relationship increasingly fruitful. (Genesis 1:28)

Equip us to honor marriage and guard the sacredness of our sexual intimacy. (Hebrews 13:4 MSG)

Marriage is a profound mystery (no wonder we don't always understand one another!); help us reflect the love between Christ and the church, united as one flesh, with love and respect for each other. (Ephesians 5:31–33)

In our lovemaking, may we be naked and vulnerable with one another, knowing no shame. (Genesis 2:25)

May our love be utterly sensual, with kisses more delightful than wine, an eagerness to hurry away together, and the security of knowing that we belong to each other. (Song of Songs 1:2–4; 7:10)

May we always see each other—even when we feel unappealing or unworthy—as beautiful and flawless. May we desire each other with a love that burns like a mighty flame that cannot be quenched. (Song of Songs 4:7; 8:6–7)

Handling Money

My wife's credit card got stolen,
but I haven't reported it yet. The thief
spends much less than she did.

Marie collapsed onto her sofa, bitter tears stinging her eyes. She didn't want to be so angry with her husband, but she couldn't help it. Roger was being an ogre.

This wasn't the first time they had squabbled over a financial decision. Marie hadn't seen the tension coming—she and Roger hadn't even *talked* about money when they were dating—but over the years it became increasingly clear that they had very different opinions about how and when to spend money. And this one was a biggie.

Roger had uprooted their family to pursue a new job in a city where they knew literally no one. Marie had been supportive of the move—a support that turned to downright excitement when she found her dream house. It was in a great neighborhood near the beach, surrounded by families with children, and it was affordable. Marie couldn't wait to make it their home.

But Roger wouldn't even *look* at the house! Sure, they had the money to buy it, but it was *too* nice, he said—much nicer than the house his new boss lived in. Buying that house wouldn't seem humble. It would look . . . proud. Showy, even.

Marie had tried to be brave. Privately, though, she grieved. She knew Ephesians 5:21, that husbands and wives should "submit to one another out of reverence for Christ," but why did it feel like *she* was always the one sacrificing her dreams? The more Marie thought about losing her dream house, the madder she got. Who knew that two *Christians* could fight so much about *money*?

A Tool, a Test, and a Testimony

Jesus might not have been surprised by Marie's frustration. He knew financial decision making would be tricky for us— which may be why he talked about money more than any other single issue.

The Bible contains more than twenty-three hundred references to money and possessions, passages that can help us understand what money is and how we should use it.[1]

For one thing, Scripture says, money is temporal. (To paraphrase 1 Timothy 6:7, "You can't take it with you.") It's not a measure of success, a guarantee of future security, or a way to find freedom from fear. Instead, the biblical perspective is that money is a tool, a test, and a testimony.

Our money is a tool that ultimately belongs to God.[2] We simply use it to accomplish a broader objective, whether we're buying new sneakers or putting cash in the offering plate. As we consider our spending patterns, we need to ask, *Are we using our money—our tool—the way God wants us to?*

> Our money is a tool that ultimately belongs to God. We simply use it to accomplish a broader objective.

Money is also a test of our faithfulness. "No one can serve two masters," Jesus says. "Either you will hate the one and love the other, or you will be devoted to the one and despise the other. You cannot serve both God and money."[3] How we handle money reveals a lot about our priorities. *Who, or what, are we serving?*

And finally, money speaks volumes about what we value or believe. "Let your light shine before others," Jesus says, "that they may see your good deeds and glorify your Father in heaven."[4] People can see, to some extent, that the way we spend our money—and everything from the houses we live in to the hobbies we pursue—sends a message. *Do our spending and giving habits bring glory to God? What is our financial testimony?*

The tool, test, and testimony outlook on money isn't something I invented. I learned it from a financial expert named Ron Blue, with whom I was privileged to write several books, including one designed to help married couples talk about—and manage—their money.[5] "There's no such thing as a money problem in marriage," Ron told me. "Instead, what looks like money trouble is almost always symptomatic of something else, and when couples understand the true purpose of money, they are much better equipped to communicate about how to handle it."

The Best Worst Wedding Gift Ever

Robbie and I have relied on the tool-test-testimony questions to help us make many decisions. Even more than that, though, we remain grateful to my folks for giving us what we thought at the time was the worst wedding present ever.

When we were engaged, my parents sent us to a Christian Financial Concepts seminar as a wedding gift. During the weekend, we learned all sorts of commonsense principles about money management, including the value of saving, the importance of staying out of debt, and the need to have a spending plan (which I now realize was just a gentler way to say "budget").

We put these principles into practice by tracking our expenses over a period of three months. That gave us a handle on our spending patterns so we could come up with a workable budget, one that covered everything from rent and utilities to clothing and food to the amount we wanted to set aside for replacing our cars, since the seminar leaders had us scared straight about going into debt for a "depreciating asset."[6]

Robbie knew I'd need help (I'm an "if it's there, we can spend it" gal), so we implemented an envelope system to keep us on track, literally stuffing our disposable income for each pay period into envelopes marked Food, Clothes, Entertainment, Gas, and—my personal favorite—Miscellaneous. I could never make the grocery or entertainment money last until the next paycheck, so by the time our fourth child was born, I'd steal the last of the cash from the gas envelope and make the kids walk to the pizza place on the corner for dinner.

We learned stuff at the seminar that financial planners don't always cover—stuff like the value of having a joint bank account (becoming "one" in every aspect of our lives, including our finances), and of not "hiding" purchases from each other. We agreed to discuss anything that cost more than fifty dollars. At the time, that number felt significant; today's couples will likely define *significant* differently. The point isn't the amount as much as it is to build discipline into your spending and, more importantly, to have clear communication about financial expectations, desires, and spending decisions.

We also talked about the merits of tithing. God doesn't "need" our money; the Bible says he already owns everything.[7] Instead, he commands us to give because it's a way of acknowledging him as our provider, of saying that it's not our exceptional brains or hard work or clever investing that enables us to accumulate wealth. The command to give is a reminder that we are where we are because God has given us all that we have. Giving shines the spotlight on God.

Not only that, but giving frees us from financial worry and fear. When Robbie and I began tithing (giving 10 percent of our income to our church and a handful of parachurch ministries), we decided to take God at his word—to believe him when he promised to supply all our needs.[8] As a result, we didn't have to live with a knot in our gut when the water heater broke or the stock market tanked. We could trust that our heavenly Father knew what we needed—even before we thought to pray about our situation.[9]

Looking back at our newlywed days, I can't fully explain the blessing that came with a commitment to tithing. Like many other upside-down teachings in Scripture (the first will be last; you must lose your life to save it), generosity is mysterious. When we give money away, we always have less

> *Giving may temporarily limit our options, but it opens the door to a life marked by so much more.*

of it. But after four decades of this mysterious upside-down living, we've found this to be true: giving may temporarily limit our options, but it opens the door to a life marked by so much more.

The Power of Unity

No matter how much money you have or how skilled you are at managing it, there will always be unlimited ways to allocate limited resources. Put another way, you never have enough money for all the stuff you want. Which can create conflict.

Robbie and I have tried to make wise decisions—using everything from the tool-test-testimony matrix to the cash-in-the-envelope system—but sometimes we've hit a brick wall. One of us (okay, usually me) will feel like we ought to buy something; the other one will not see it as a need (or even a want). When that happens—when one of us isn't on board with a purchase or an investment—we take it as a sign that the discussion should be tabled. We need to take time to get additional information, seek the counsel of others, and pray, even if it means missing out on what looks like a great deal.

As Robbie often reminds me, "There will always be another great deal."

What matters to God more than our financial portfolio is our unity. He longs for us to be "perfectly united in mind and thought," to be "one in spirit and of one mind" as we value each other above ourselves.[10]

We get that. Unity is amazing. But in marriage, there will be times when we just disagree—especially about money.

What matters to God more than our financial portfolio is our unity.

And honestly? When I heard Marie's story about not getting her dream house, I understood her frustration and anger. I've asked myself the same thing sometimes: *Why do I have to yield* my *desires to Robbie's?*

Much has been made—and misunderstood—about Ephesians 5:22, the verse in which God calls women to submit to their husbands. And while there is infinitely more that can be said on this topic, I'll give you the short version of where I've landed.

I can yield to Robbie because I know he values my opinions. He doesn't make decisions without taking my perspective—and my good—into account. Having read all of Ephesians 5, he lives it out well, using his authority to serve me the way Christ does for the church.

Even more than that, I can yield to Robbie—and delight in doing so—because I know he is accountable to God. I actually love the freedom that comes when Robbie makes the call on something. If I've prayed about a decision and added my thoughts to the mix, I can release the outcome, knowing I've done the job God gave me to do and that he can be trusted to work in all things, even decisions I may not agree with, for our good.[11]

And finally, I can yield because Christ did so first.

We may not understand exactly why he gave up his authority and yielded to the Father, but he did so—willingly—and that changed everything.

Again, there is much more we could say on the subject of decision making and the different roles of husbands and wives, but if you long for unity in your finances but aren't there yet, trust God to help. Ask him to give you wisdom and grace as you talk with each other (use the questions in the "Reflect" section to jump-start your conversation), and be open to what the Holy Spirit may want to show you as you allow Scripture to shape your perspective.

That's actually what happened with Marie. As she fell onto her sofa, angry beyond words over Roger's refusal to even consider buying her dream house, her eyes fell on the Bible that was open beside her.

"I find nothing wrong with this man."

The words come from Luke 23:4 (NLT), where Pontius Pilate tells the crowd that Jesus doesn't deserve to be crucified, but Marie knew God was speaking to her. She had a whole list of her husband's faults—even his humility had a place in her record of where he was wrong—but God saw things differently. He approved of Roger.

Marie felt her rancor evaporating. And as she continued to study the Bible in a more intentional way, reading verses like Proverbs 2:17 (which describes marriage, not as a union where one person dominates the other, but as a covenant partnership) and Proverbs 31:11–12 (which talks about a husband having confidence in his wife and a wife bringing him good rather than harm), her prayers started to shift. She still wanted to live in a beautiful home, but more than that, she wanted Roger to know she was on his team. At the end of the day, their relationship mattered more than any spending decision. Together, she and Roger could ask God for wisdom. And together, they could trust him to provide—knowing, as Ephesians 3:20 puts it, that God is able to do "immeasurably more than all we ask or imagine"—even when it comes to deciding where we should live.

Remember

God will meet all your needs according to the riches of his glory in Christ Jesus. (Philippians 4:19)

Reflect

Set aside a time (a date night or a weekend) to talk with your spouse about your finances. How have your different backgrounds shaped your perspectives on money? Are you comfortable with your spending habits and investment strategy? Your debt? Your giving? What do your financial habits say about what you believe?

Think about your financial dreams and goals. Share those with each other, as well as any fears or worries you have. Confess any areas where you've let fear or greed dictate your decisions and ask God to help you put your hope in him as your provider.

God promises to meet all your needs. He longs to bless you—abundantly—so you can be generous in every way.[12] Invite God into the conversation, asking him to grant unity and wisdom in decision making.

Respond

Heavenly Father,

As we talk about money, make us like-minded, loving, and united in spirit and mind. Don't let us be selfish or vain; rather, give us the humility to value each other above ourselves. (Philippians 2:2–3)

May we be trustworthy in handling worldly wealth, devoting ourselves to serving God instead of being mastered by money. (Luke 16:11–13)

As we think about where we should live, may it be a peaceful and secure dwelling, an undisturbed place where our family and guests will experience relaxation and rest. (Isaiah 32:18)

Don't let us wear ourselves out trying to get rich; grant us the wisdom to gather money little by little and make it grow. (Proverbs 23:4; 13:11)

(For a wife) Help me understand and support my husband, submitting to his leadership and honoring him in the way I think about and handle money. (Ephesians 5:22–24 MSG)

(For a husband) Help me go all out in loving my wife—not by domineering but by cherishing her perspective on our finances. May I be more focused on giving than getting, saying and doing things that bring out the best in her. (Ephesians 5:25–28 MSG)

As we talk about tithing, let us remember that everything we have—including our ability to accumulate and give away money—comes from you. (1 Chronicles 29:12–14)

Protect us from arrogance and the temptation to put our hope in material wealth. You richly provide everything for our enjoyment; equip us to be rich in good deeds, generous, and willing to share. (1 Timothy 6:17–18)

Keep our lives free from the love of money. Teach us to be content with what we have, secure in the knowledge that you will never leave us. (Hebrews 13:5)

Bless us abundantly, so that in all things at all times, having all that we need, we may abound in every good work. Enrich us in every way so we can be generous on every occasion and bring glory to you. (2 Corinthians 9:8–11)

Help us be wise financial planners, counting the cost of any undertaking and being intentional about our giving, making decisions thoughtfully and without reluctance, since you love a cheerful giver. (Luke 14:28; 2 Corinthians 9:7)

Teach us not to worry about material things—things like what we'll eat or what we'll wear—but to seek you first, knowing that you will take care of all of our everyday needs. (Matthew 6:31–33)

Meet all our needs according to the riches of your glory in Christ Jesus. (Philippians 4:19)

CHAPTER
— *twelve* —

Serving Each Other in Love

Married life is waking up early to preheat your
spouse's car in the winter (and then taking ten
dollars out of their wallet as a tip for your services).

"Be ready to do whatever is good." "Use whatever gift you have received to serve others." "Serve one another humbly in love."[1]

The Bible overflows with instructions like these. The directives are intended for every Christian and every relationship, but nowhere does the exhortation to be quick to serve others, putting their needs and interests ahead of your own, come with more transformative power than in marriage.

Unlike other human relationships, marriage affords what can feel like a million little opportunities for service every day. Making the coffee, letting the dog out, agreeing to go to the party with your spouse's coworkers (the one you have no desire to attend)—all of these daily decisions represent a choice to live not for yourself but for your spouse. And while doing so may be hard (we are, by nature, self-centered people), the rewards can be both significant and surprising.

In the midst of what she acknowledges was a "difficult season in a very difficult year," our friend Lisa Jacobson made a conscious decision to serve her husband every day, whether that meant folding his shirts just the way he liked them (and putting them away!), planning an unexpected date night, or laughing at his corny jokes. She didn't just do these things for a week or two; Lisa embarked on a one-hundred-day "Love Challenge." She figured it would make her man happy (and it did), but what she wasn't prepared for was the impact it had on her. "The more I chose love, the more loving—and loved—I felt," she writes. "It grew into something of a game, and . . . later, as the days went on, I felt this slow renewing of pleasure and delight."[2]

We know other couples whose marriages have taken an opposite path—and in fact, research points to the disintegrating effect that self-centeredness can have on a marriage. When one spouse insists on getting their own way, it creates a climate in which impatience, resentment, and selfishness can thrive, leading to "a downward spiral into self-pity, anger, and despair, as the relationship gets eaten away to nothing."[3]

The apostle Paul wouldn't be surprised to see love flourishing in one marriage and dying out in another. "A man reaps what he sows," he wrote. "Whoever sows to please their flesh, from the flesh will reap destruction; whoever sows to please the Spirit, from the Spirit will reap eternal life. Let us not become weary in doing good, for at the proper time we will reap a harvest if we do not give up."[4]

> *Selfishness will destroy a marriage, while imitating Christ, who came not to be served but to serve, leads ultimately to a harvest of blessing.*

Put another way, selfishness (doing what pleases your flesh) will destroy a marriage, while imitating Christ, who came not to be served but to serve,[5] leads ultimately to a harvest of blessing.

Becoming Beautiful

Two months after he left his job as the head of US operations for an international organization, Davis found himself unpacking chairs for his wife, Jennie. Twenty of them. The chairs didn't technically belong to Jennie; they were for one of her interior design clients, a doctor. Being made of fine wood and leather, the chairs had been meticulously wrapped and taped, and Davis had to be careful not to damage anything. As he worked, he calculated that each one took twenty-two minutes to unpack. Twenty-two minutes. He wondered if he'd be able to finish them all in a day.

"You must do that outside!"

Davis looked up to see who was speaking. It was the doctor's wife, leaning over the reception counter, and she was clearly unhappy. "Take the chairs out," the woman repeated. "You are disrupting the customers!"

Eyeing the empty waiting room, Davis wasn't sure whether to laugh or cry. *In two months*, he thought to himself, *I've gone from being the president of a major company to being scolded for disrupting imaginary customers while I unwrap chairs for free. This is beautiful.*

You may wonder why Davis thought that doing menial labor—and getting reprimanded in the process—was beautiful. For one thing, Davis recognized that his wife had spent forty years serving him as they moved all over the country for his career, making each place a joyful home for their family. Now the opportunity to put her needs ahead of his own and help her be successful in her job felt good and right.

Not only that, but Davis realized that his identity was not rooted in having a prestigious job. Nor was he defined by his work on the chairs or by what the doctor's wife—or anyone else—said about him. Instead, Davis knew he was loved by Jesus. That was the truest thing about him. And in that, he told us, "the service of unwrapping became beautiful. Sacred even."

Knowing how much we are loved by the Lord—and that we can love others because, as 1 John 4:19 says, God loved us first—is what equips us for service. Our spouses are just like the rest of the world—imperfect and not always grateful. But when we remember how very flawed we also are, and how much we have been given (and forgiven) by God, spending ourselves on behalf of another can become a joy, not a duty. The simplest acts of service can become beautiful.

Outserve Each Other

Our contemporary culture holds a dim view of service—we'd rather be served than serve—but at some gut-instinct level, we know that putting our spouse's needs ahead of our own makes for a healthy and enjoyable marriage. Paul's counsel to husbands and wives to "submit to one another" sounds like the right thing to do.[6] But knowing the right thing to do and actually doing it are two different things. Which is why, just a few verses earlier, Paul gives us the critical how-to: "Be filled with the Spirit."[7]

Being filled with the Spirit allows us to love others in ways

> At some gut-instinct level, we know that putting our spouse's needs ahead of our own makes for a healthy and enjoyable marriage.

that don't always come naturally. It empowers us to let go of our self-centered desires and live lives marked by things like patience, goodness, gentleness, and self-control.[8] And it marks us with the same self-sacrificing humility that Jesus displayed, whether he was washing his disciples' dirty feet or, as Philippians 2:8 puts it, humbling himself and becoming "obedient to death—even death on a cross!"

This Philippians passage, with its call to "have the same mindset as Christ Jesus" (2:5)—loving as he did, pursuing unity as he did, putting others first as he did—offers a template for our relationships.[9] Early in our marriage, Robbie and I heard Dr. Tony Evans talk about what this pattern looked like in his own marriage. Having purposed to value each other's interests ahead of their own, Evans and his wife began going out of their way to help each other. At some point, Evans said, it became a contest—one he found himself losing.

"I couldn't believe it," Evans said with a laugh. "She was *outserving* me. I had to figure out how to catch up!"

Evans's message took hold in our hearts, and Robbie and I began looking for opportunities to honor each other. Robbie likes things tidy, and while I knew I couldn't match his mother's "get the dust off the top of the refrigerator" talent, the kids and I began playing "beat the buzzer" every night before he came home. I'd set the kitchen timer and we'd scramble to pick up toys and clean the counters. On my good days, I'd even rummage in my purse to find the lip gloss as Robbie's car pulled into the driveway. (And if I just lost half of the women readers, I'm sorry. But never once did I feel like I was caught in some 1950s time warp. Instead, I saw these little acts of service—and my lips, on some days—as, to use our friend Davis's word, "beautiful.")

For his part, Robbie began doing things like vacuuming my (dog-hair-and-Cheerios-infested) car or bringing me coffee—sometimes from an actual coffee shop, which he knows is my love language and counts double on the service scale, since a little part of him dies inside every time he pays for something we can get for free at home.

Somewhere along the way—we can't pinpoint when—something shifted inside us. We began to truly enjoy these tangible ways to show love and respect. It became, like our friend Lisa says, a "pleasure and a delight." And although I don't feel deserving of Robbie's tenderness, the word he uses for the way he regards me is *cherish*, and when I noticed that a book by that title had been published, I grabbed it.

"Millions of couples," writes author Gary Thomas, "have pledged 'to love and to cherish, till death do us part.'" Most of us understand the love part and the implied vow to serve and commit to one another, but it is the act of cherishing, Thomas says, that "turns marriage from an obligation into a delight. It lifts marriage above a commitment to a precious priority."[10]

Serving your spouse—cherishing them as precious—looks different in every marriage. Bob took his children to garage sales on Saturday mornings, not because they needed more stuff, but because it gave his wife, Anne, a chance to have the house to herself at the start of the weekend. Whit turns the bed down every night and puts his wife, Susan's, iPad on her pillow, since he knows she loves to read. I stopped wearing ruffles (after having an umpteen hundred of them on my puffball of a wedding dress) when I learned (later) that they don't appeal to Robbie.

None of these things are "grand" gestures. They may go unmarked by everyone but our spouse. And yet in a social media age when everyone wants to be seen and noticed, it is exactly these little gifts of time, these self-sacrificing kindnesses, that kindle lasting love in a marriage.

> *In a social media age when everyone wants to be seen and noticed, it is exactly gifts of time and self-sacrificing kindnesses that kindle lasting love in a marriage.*

"Real romance," writes Ann Voskamp, "isn't measured by how viral any wedding proposal goes—and viral is closely associated with sickness—but it's the moments of self-forgetfulness: Setting the table at the end of a long day and rustling up some hearty dish for those who have your heart, and then—without any cameras rolling or soundtracks playing—clearing the plates to make your own love perfectly clear—this is the way of robust romance."[11]

Robust romance. Isn't that what we all want? The way to get there isn't through grasping; it is through yielding. Yielding our plans, our desires, our very self—and submitting out of reverence for the One who is Love himself to the one whom we cherish.

Remember

Serve one another humbly in love. (Galatians 5:13)

Reflect

We love because God first loved us. The more we soak up this truth, the more our love will increase and overflow for our spouse. Think about your own awareness of God's love for you. Do you sense his delight? Do you feel forgiven? Can you trace a link between your relationship with the Lord and your desire to serve and honor your spouse?

Describe a time when you felt especially cherished by your spouse. How did it impact your relationship? Are there specific things you can do this week—even if they go unnoticed—to outserve one another?

Philippians 2:6–7 says that Jesus was equal to God, but he didn't use that to his advantage; rather, he made himself nothing. Ask the Holy Spirit to fill you afresh—to give you the spirit and mind of the Lord—and to know that your worth comes not from any status or position but in your identity as God's beloved.

Respond

Heavenly Father,

Show us how to encourage one another and build each other up. (1 Thessalonians 5:11)

Do not let us get fatigued as we do good to each other, since at the right time we will reap a crop if we don't give up. Right now, therefore, every time we get the chance, let us work for the benefit of our spouse, the one closest to us. (Galatians 6:9 MSG)

Equip us to love one another with genuine affection and take delight in honoring each other. (Romans 12:10 NLT)

Help us serve one another humbly in love. (Galatians 5:13)

Let us use whatever gifts we have received from you to serve each other, faithfully stewarding your grace in its various forms. (1 Peter 4:10)

You came not to be served but to serve and to give your life as a ransom for many. Teach us to serve each other like that, giving our lives—our time, our resources, our energy, our love—sacrificially to one another. (Mark 10:45)

May we be joyful in hope, patient in affliction, and faithful in prayer, always sharing with each other as we have need. (Romans 12:12–13)

Prompt us to do good, to be rich in good deeds, and to be generous to each other and willing to share. (1 Timothy 6:18)

Let us consider how we may spur one another on toward love and good deeds, not giving up meeting together, as some are in the habit of doing, but encouraging one another—and all the more as we see the Day approaching. (Hebrews 10:24–25)

Whatever we do for each other, may we work at it with all our heart, as working for you, Lord. (Colossians 3:23)

Don't let us be selfish or conceited. Rather, grant us the humility to value one another above ourselves, not looking to our own personal interests but to the interests and needs of our spouse. (Philippians 2:3–4)

Fill us with your Spirit; make us thankful; teach us to submit to one another out of reverence for Christ. (Ephesians 5:18–21)

Having Fun Together

*The next time your wife gets angry, drape
a towel over her shoulders (like a cape)
and say, "Now you're super angry."
Maybe she'll laugh.
Maybe you'll die.*

"Marry someone who makes you laugh."

That's the advice Susan gave to all five of her kids. She hoped (and prayed) they'd find mates who loved Jesus, who were thoughtful and kind, and who came from loving and supportive families, but the banner she stretched over all of these attributes was that their marriages would be marked by laughter and joy.

You can imagine Susan's delight when she opened her mailbox one day and found a letter from her son John.

He had met a young woman, and while the letter was short on details, it told Susan everything she needed to know.

> Dear Mom,
>> She makes me laugh!
>> What more can I say?
>
>> Love,
>> John Jr.

Sure enough, within a year, peals of laughter were accompanied by those of wedding bells.

Proverbs 17:22 reads, "A cheerful heart is good medicine." And while having a good sense of humor or a cheerful outlook may not cure all that ails you, more and more scientific studies point to the mental and physical health benefits that come with laughter and joy.

For instance, researchers at the Mayo Clinic found that a good laugh doesn't just lighten our load mentally; it actually induces physical changes in our bodies, some of which have long-term effects.[1] Laughter releases endorphins, relieves stress, and soothes tension through improved circulation and muscle relaxation. It stimulates our hearts and lungs with oxygen. It combats depression and anxiety and increases self-esteem. And the positive thoughts that trigger laughter also release neuropeptides that improve our immune systems.

Perhaps the best news about laughter—at least in terms

of how it can impact our marriage—is that it increases our sense of personal satisfaction. "Laughter," according to the Mayo Clinic staff, can "make it easier to cope with difficult situations" and help us "connect with other people."[2]

A good laugh doesn't just lighten our load mentally; it actually induces physical changes in our bodies, some of which have long-term effects.

Some people, of course, are naturally more lighthearted than others. My mom's first date with John was to the movie *King Kong*, and when the time came for them to get married, John thought it only made sense for his adult son to don a gorilla suit and kidnap Mom, in a full-length white wedding gown, from the dance floor in front of 180 guests—setting the stage for a dramatic "damsel in distress" rescue by the tuxedo-clad groom. With such a comical and adventurous beginning, I wasn't surprised when, a few years later, a friend texted a photo of the happy couple lying flat on their backs in the snow. At first I thought they'd been shot. But then I zoomed in on the pic and realized that Mom and John—two septuagenarians—were out there making snow angels.

Don't Let Stress Steal Your Joy

Gorillas on the guest list or not, the union of husband and wife is, as we're often reminded at weddings, "intended by God for their mutual joy."[3] God wants us to enjoy married life—to have fun together. But even the most upbeat, well-suited couples will go through hard seasons, months (even years) when we need to guard against joy stealers like stress and fatigue.

Robbie and I were thrilled at the prospect of starting a family (and little ones certainly do make you laugh!), but nothing in the parenting classes or books we devoured prepared us for the physical exhaustion we'd face during the baby and toddler years, particularly since Robbie traveled during the week for his job. And it didn't get any easier as the kids became more independent. My stint in youth ministry had convinced me that teens are creative and fun, and we looked forward to having four of them under our roof. As it turned out, teens *are* creative and fun, but as I wrote in *Praying the Scriptures for Your Teens*, there were plenty of days when "our spirits were heavy. The list of what-ifs and worries—safety on the road, substance abuse, eating disorders, anxiety, sexual purity, spiritual doubt—seemed limitless." It felt, I said, like "whack-a-mole" parenting; no sooner would we finish praying about one thing than another would pop its head out of the hole.[4]

Parenting is not, obviously, the only thing that can put stress on a marriage. Sickness, financial struggles, job concerns, aging parents, mental health issues, extended family dynamics, and any number of other factors can leave us feeling preoccupied, tense, worried, or tired. Throw in the not-always-uplifting effects of social media—including the newish and very real habit of "doomscrolling" (bingeing on negative news)—and we might not even remember our last good belly laugh or time when we had fun together.

In his book *Have Serious Fun*, our friend Jim Burns tells an all-too-familiar story. Jim and his wife, Cathy, were facing some stressful challenges at work, two of their adult kids had boomeranged home, COVID-19 was changing the business and social networking landscape, and the nightly newsfeeds showed a divided and angry nation. They felt maxed out and upside down. "It was time," Jim writes, "for a break and some fun."

Jim and Cathy got in their car and drove to the beach. The shops and restaurants were closed, but they didn't care. They spent time walking, napping, laughing, watching the sunsets, and focusing on each other. It wasn't a long getaway, but as they drove home, they agreed that they each felt refreshed.

"The problems of our world hadn't disappeared," Jim says, "but that time to play gave us the energy and courage to step back into the not-so-fun moments of life."[5]

How to Get Serious about Having Fun

So how do we do that? How do we *intentionally* make space to play, to enjoy one another, to laugh—both to refresh our marriage and to equip us to stay in the game?

You could order a book of dad jokes. I did that one year for Robbie's birthday, and we shared a chuckle or two. In retrospect, though, a better idea is to talk to our actual Dad—the One who *wants* us to be joyful—and ask for his help. We can borrow King David's words to shape our prayer: "Make known to us the path of life; fill us with joy in your presence, with eternal pleasures at your right hand."[6]

As we pray—as we invite God to show us how to get serious about having fun—we should ask ourselves an obvious question: *What do we like to do?* Having fun looks different for everyone. Our friends Susan and Randy love to go birding; Robbie and I aren't even sure what this hobby entails, other than binoculars and some mosquito repellant.

> *As we pray, we should ask ourselves an obvious question: What do we like to do?*

In their book *Creative Love*, Audrey and Jeremy Roloff dish up all sorts of ideas on everything from celebrating holidays to planning memorable date nights to trying new things and embarking on adventures together. Some adventures (wake up early and watch the sunrise, take a dance class, go on a tandem bike ride) don't call for much money or planning; others (create a personalized scavenger hunt based on your own love story, set up a backyard movie theater) are more involved.

Robbie and I liked a lot of the Roloffs' suggestions, but perhaps the most valuable takeaway was their advice on responding to unexpected, less-than-fun circumstances with patience and grace. "Jer and I learned early in our marriage," Audrey says, "to expect something to go wrong on every adventure. That way, when the wrong thing happens, we smile and claim it as 'the thing,' and it keeps us from getting frazzled . . . It prevents 'the thing' from turning into conflict."[7]

As you think about date nights and adventures, take turns making plans. And as our daughters told us when they were teens, "Don't yuck each other's yum." Just because something doesn't sound fun to *you* doesn't mean it won't be fun if you try it—at least once—with your spouse. Robbie rolled his eyes when I bought a pickleball net and handed him the sidewalk chalk to map out a court in our driveway (measuring stuff being more in his strike zone than mine). We invited another couple to play and—maybe because the driveway slants and is ringed by some particularly prickly holly bushes—we laughed until our stomachs hurt. (Plus, Robbie turned out to be really good at the game, which made him decide it wasn't so bad.)

Trying a new sport, taking a dance class, going birding together—"these things might not seem," as author and theologian Phylicia Masonheimer puts it, "like the heavyweight actions of biblical joy. But if they draw you closer together, isn't that glorifying to God? Laughter bonds us with others. Shared laughter can bond you and your spouse in a special way, even if the activity isn't super spiritual."[8]

Likewise, praying about having fun doesn't seem as important as asking God to help us handle conflict or be kind to each other. But when we stop to consider how much God values joy—how often, in Scripture, he says he wants our joy to overflow or how he longs to fill our mouths with laughter—we can only conclude that he is utterly serious about joy.[9]

Have fun with your spouse. Be intentional about creating a climate in which laughter can thrive. And whether you're naturally funny or not (and if not, that's okay; the world needs regular people who *appreciate* funny people), ask God to help you rejoice. Jesus came, after all, to tell us how to live so his joy would be in us and our joy would be full.[10]

Remember

A cheerful disposition is good for your health;

gloom and doom leave you bone-tired.

(Proverbs 17:22 MSG)

Reflect

God is a God of laughter. He rejoices over us and longs for our marriages to reflect his delight as we take joy in one another. Have things like stress or fatigue been stealing your joy? What would it take for you to be more intentional about having fun? Are there things you need to let go of in order to make space to play, get away, or just relax together? What does fun look like to you?

Talk with your spouse about the value of laughter and shared adventures. Ask God to open your eyes to some ways you can enjoy each other, even if you are in a challenging season. Decide on one fun thing you can do together this week, and trust God to fill you with joy.

Respond

Heavenly Father,
Fill our mouths with laughter and our lips with shouts of joy. (Job 8:21)

May we be glad and rejoice before you; may we be happy and joyful. (Psalm 68:3)

Show us how to thank you, God, from a full heart and how to write the book on your wonders. May we whistle, laugh, and jump for joy; may we sing your song, High God. (Psalm 9:1–2 MSG)

Clothe us with strength and dignity; may we laugh at the days to come. (Proverbs 31:25)

When "the thing" happens in the midst of our adventure, remind us not to get frazzled since wisdom yields patience and it is to one's glory to overlook an offense. (Proverbs 19:11)

Let us run loose and free, celebrating your great work, every bone in our bodies laughing, singing, "God, there's no one like you!" (Psalm 35:9 MSG)

Cause us to keep your commands and remain in your love so your joy will be in us and our joy will be complete. (John 15:10–11)

Even when our lives feel dry or like we are walking through the Valley of Weeping, help us trust you to make our marriage a place of refreshing springs, one clothed with your blessings. (Psalm 84:6 NLT)

May our marriage reflect the joy of the Lord. Let's say it again: may we rejoice! (Philippians 4:4)

Make known to us the path of life; fill us with joy in your presence, with eternal pleasures at your right hand. (Psalm 16:11)

We love you, Lord. We believe in you. Fill us with an inexpressible and glorious joy as we consider the end result of our faith, the salvation of our souls. (1 Peter 1:8–9)

Fill our mouths with laughter! Let others look at us and say, "The Lord has done great things for them.".You have done great things for us, and we are filled with joy. (Psalm 126:2–3)

Parenting Priorities

I saw a sign that said, "Watch for children."
I said to myself, "That sounds like a fair trade."

A cross-stitched sampler hung on the wall in my growing-up kitchen. "The greatest thing a man can do for his children," the needlework read, "is to love their mother."

As a teen, I figured my mother had hung it there like a motivational poster of sorts for my dad, the way I taped signs to the fridge as my birthday approached: "Ten shopping days left."

Now, more than thirty years later, I realize the power in that one single sentence—and that (as my mom knew) the words cut both ways. As dads and as moms, the greatest thing we can do for our kids is to model Christ's love—and put his John 13:34 command into practice—by loving one another.

The thing is, though, most of us don't. We don't prioritize our marriage relationship—at least not consistently and intentionally—in ways that keep our focus on each other. Instead, we center our lives around our children. Babies and toddlers demand our physical energy and attention, and

The greatest thing we can do for our kids is to model Christ's love—and put his John 13:34 command into practice—by loving one another.

then as they grow and become more independent, our kids continue to captivate our hearts and our minds. They can even become idols of sorts—either because they are so cute/talented/smart/athletic that they make us *proud*, or because their behavior/friendships/lifestyle choices/work habits make us *anxious*. One way or another, our children can fill the radar screen of our devotion, pushing our spouse (and our marriage) to the outer edges of the field.

I'm not pointing fingers. Trust me, Robbie and I have been the proud/anxious/all-consumed parents more times than either of us cares to admit. We made plenty of rookie (and not-so-rookie) mistakes—and now that we're empty nesters, we're finding out what Mitch Robbins (played by Billy Crystal) meant in the movie *City Slickers* when he said we'd spend our days "looking for the ultimate in soft yogurt and muttering, 'How come the kids don't call?'"[1] But as we look back on our parenting journey, child-focused and neurotic as it often was, I'm convinced we did two things right.

First, we let our kids see us pray. We knew we didn't have all the answers, and as we openly acknowledged our dependence on God, our children learned to look past our weaknesses and recognize God's strength and provision for our family. Seeing a weak and flawed earthly parent talking to a powerful and perfect heavenly Parent can give kids a greater sense of security than any family love, friendship circle, or financial wealth could ever provide.

> As we openly acknowledged our dependence on God, our children learned to look past our weaknesses and recognize God's strength and provision for our family.

The second thing we did—the thing that gave our kids a greater sense of security and family stability than anything else—was to ignore them. Not always, of course, but for about ten or fifteen minutes every day.

Happy Marriage, Healthy Kids

Robbie and I had four kids in six years. We didn't live near either of our families when the last two were born, and since we were keenly aware of our need for help and advice, we were grateful when some friends invited us to join them for a parenting class. We gathered with a handful of other couples—all of whom had little ones like we did—and explored what the Bible had to say about all sorts of topics, from character development to effective discipline. The course proved eye-opening as a parenting resource, but it was transformational for our marriage as well.

Warning us about the dangers of what they called "child-centered parenting," the leaders encouraged us to prioritize the husband-wife relationship with things like weekly date nights and "couch time." We'd never heard of couch time, but we started doing it right away. Every night when Robbie came home from work, we enjoyed ten or fifteen minutes, just us, sitting on the sofa, talking. The kids were dying to jump all over Robbie—we all were—but they knew better than to interrupt.

At least three things happened as a result of those handful of minutes. First, I felt special, knowing that whatever I had to say about the day, no matter how mundane, mattered to Robbie. Second, the children got a nightly witness of what prioritizing a marriage looks like. And third, in a side effect I did not fully appreciate at the time, they gained the sense that our marriage—and by extension our family—was stable.

Our kids are grown now, with kids of their own. Like many of their peers, both Mom and Dad work outside the home. This can make "just us" time harder to implement; it's natural to want to focus on the children instead of each other when you haven't seen them all day. But we're encouraging our adult children to make this one-on-one time part of their family routine—maybe not right when they get home from work, but at some point during the evening (or on weekends) when the children can see what is happening.

Robbie and I can still picture our four little "monkeys," giggling and peeking around the corner into the living room and stage-whispering to each other, "Shhh! This is Mom and Dad's time!" They had no idea what we were talking about; that wasn't what mattered. What mattered was that they knew their parents were focused on each other—and they loved it. And while we didn't know it back then, what we were doing had a profound impact on both their sense of security as children and their future happiness in their own marriages.

Plenty of research points to the link between destructive behaviors in a marriage and the negative impact they can have on a child's emotional or physical health. But the opposite is also true. The good things—things like showing honor to your spouse and giving them a healthy dose of affection—can help kids "feel more secure and stable at home," says psychologist and marriage expert Susan Orenstein, "allowing them to enjoy being a kid."[2] Not only that, but when we model such healthy behaviors toward one another—whether it's through kind words, physical touch, or a genuine interest in what our partner is saying—we provide a barometer for what an eventual spouse should look like. Our kids will be drawn to people who evidence similar qualities because it's what they know.[3]

In other words, my mom's cross-stitched sampler was

right: as parents, the greatest thing we can do for our children is to love each other.

More Is Caught Than Taught

The importance of prioritizing our marriage when it comes to how we parent our children is not surprising—not when we remember that God designed marriage to be a picture of his love relationship with us and that he established marriage before he gave Abraham (or anyone else) any promises about what he would do through the families that came from the union of husband and wife.

So how are we doing when it comes to loving, serving, and honoring one another? Are we living in a way that reflects God's love for his church? Are we laying the groundwork, through the preeminence of our marriage, for successful family dynamics and thriving communities?

It has been said that more is caught than taught, and if we want our children to grow up and enjoy healthy marriages of their own—as well as have a love relationship with the Lord—we need to let them catch us loving each other. We need to let them see us speaking kindly to each other, even when we disagree. We need to let them hear us praising one another, even if it's for something as routine as cooking dinner or submitting tax forms on time. And we need to let them know that we know we're not perfect.

Many parents struggle under the burden of wanting to "get it all right." Wanting to set a good example. To have limitless patience. To keep our tempers under control. And when we don't—when we blow it and say or do something we wish we could take back—we worry that we've ruined our kids.

In reality, though, we'll never be perfect parents, just like we'll never have a perfect marriage. And the more our kids see us asking for—and extending—forgiveness, the more they'll begin to understand and appreciate the power of the gospel. The more they'll be drawn to the God who covers their ugliest flaws and offenses with the beauty of his mercy and grace. The more equipped they will be to grow up and enter into marriages and families of their own, joining their voices with those who have gone before:

> *The more our kids see us asking for—and extending—forgiveness, the more they'll begin to understand and appreciate the power of the gospel.*

> We will not hide them from their descendants;
>> We will tell the next generation
> the praiseworthy deeds of the LORD,
>> his power, and the wonders he has done . . .
> so the next generation would know them,
>> even the children yet to be born,
>> and they in turn would tell their children.

> Then they would put their trust in God
> and would not forget his deeds
> but would keep his commands.[4]

We all want to build healthy families and raise our children—the next generation—to know and love Jesus. Loving our spouse is the place where that starts.

Remember ─────────────────

One generation commends your works to another;
they tell of your mighty acts. (Psalm 145:4)

Reflect ─────────────────

In the ancient world, sons were often a measure of a family's worth. And it can be easy, even today, to associate our value with our children—how many kids we have, how successful they are, how engaged we are in their lives through schooling, sports, family time, and so forth. Not only does this attitude open the door to idol worship, but anchoring our identity in our children can have painful consequences for our marriage as well.

Take some time to reflect on your own family habits. Do you regularly put your children and their needs ahead of your spouse? Do you struggle with the pressure to "get it all right" in your parenting or your marriage? Do your children see you extending—and receiving—forgiveness? Do they know you pray regularly?

Ask God to reveal any areas where your family priorities might be misaligned. Surrender your habits and desires to him, trusting the Holy Spirit to help you honor your spouse and release any pressure you feel to be perfect. God longs to reveal his love through your marriage; commit to partnering with him through your prayers as you trust him to bless and protect your family.

Respond

Heavenly Father,

Bless our family and keep us. Make your face shine on us and be gracious to us; turn your face toward us and give us peace. (Numbers 6:24–26)

May our children see the gospel reflected in our marriage as we submit to one another out of reverence for you and treat one another with love and respect. (Ephesians 5:21, 33)

Don't let us exasperate our children; rather, help us bring them up in the training and instruction of the Lord. (Ephesians 6:4)

Help us teach our children to love you with all they've got! May we have your commands inside us and get them inside our children, talking about them from the time we get up in the morning to when we fall into bed at night. (Deuteronomy 6:5–7 MSG)

In our home, may we talk about the glorious splendor of your majesty and meditate on your works, one generation commending you to another. (Psalm 145:4–5)

Be faithful to us as your covenant people. Let our descendants be known among the nations. May all who see our offspring acknowledge that we are your people and that you have blessed us. (Isaiah 61:9)

Equip us to tell the next generation about your praiseworthy deeds, your power, and the wonders you have done. (Psalm 78:4)

You are the Good Shepherd. Watch over our family, gathering our children in your arms and gently leading us as we raise them. (Isaiah 40:11)

Pour out your Spirit on our offspring, your blessing on our descendants. (Isaiah 44:3)

Grant that we might partake in the covenant you established with Abraham. Let us obey you wholeheartedly and bless others through our family. (Genesis 22:18)

Bonus: A Dozen Prayers for Your Children:

Open _____'s eyes and turn them from darkness to light, and from the power of Satan to God, so that they may receive forgiveness of sins and a place among those who are sanctified by faith in Christ. (Acts 26:18)

Let _____ take refuge in you; may they ever sing for joy. Spread your protection over them; surround them with your favor as with a shield. (Psalm 5:11–12)

May _____ grow as Jesus did, in wisdom and stature, and in favor with God and man. (Luke 2:52)

Prompt _____ to obey us and honor us, as you command, so that it may go well with them and they may enjoy a long life. (Ephesians 6:1–3)

Make _____ kind and compassionate to their siblings and friends, forgiving others just as Christ forgave them. (Ephesians 4:32)

May _____ do good, be rich in good deeds, be generous toward their siblings and friends, and always be willing to share. (1 Timothy 6:18)

Do immeasurably more for _____ than all we could ever ask or imagine. Be glorified in _____'s life. (Ephesians 3:20)

Instruct _____ and teach them in the way they should go; counsel them with your loving eye on them. (Psalm 32:8)

Bless _____ abundantly, so that in all things at all times, having all that they need, they will abound in every good work. (2 Corinthians 9:8)

May your favor rest on _____; establish the work of their hands and make their efforts successful. (Psalm 90:17)

Fill _____ with all joy and peace as they trust in you so that they may overflow with hope by the power of the Holy Spirit. (Romans 15:13)

May _____ daily grow in the grace and knowledge of our Lord and Savior Jesus Christ. (2 Peter 3:18)

CHAPTER
fifteen

Making Good Friends

*I was glad when they lifted the Covid-19 restrictions
and said we could get together with friends without
any issues. But then my husband reminded me,
"We don't have any friends without any issues."*

*"In the name of God, I, Robbie, take you, Jodie, to be my wife,
to have and to hold from this day forward, for better, for worse,
for richer, for poorer, in sickness and in health, to love and to
cherish, until we are parted by death. This is my solemn vow."*

I loved hearing Robbie say those words on our wedding
day, and I loved hearing our children recite the same vows at
their weddings. I love it when *any* couple promises to have
and to hold one another—forever.

But there's another vow in the marriage ceremony I love

almost as much. Before the officiant addresses the couple, he or she looks at the wedding guests: "Will all of you witnessing these promises do all in your power to uphold these two persons in their marriage?"

It's a great question, and I have to curb my enthusiasm every time it's asked. I want to shout the answer—*We will!*—but out of respect for my more appropriate husband, I don't. I just say it. Loudly.

This vow affirms the ages-old idea that Christian marriage is rooted in community. No couple can go it alone. We are all meant to function and thrive as part of the larger body of Christ.

No couple can go it alone. We are all meant to function and thrive as part of the larger body of Christ.

Sadly, though, this experience of community connection is growing increasingly less common. Today, we can have digital connections with hundreds of people and yet live our whole lives without true community. We can work from home, shop from home, even (thank you, pandemic) do church from home. We may think of these things as normal, if not wonderful, modern conveniences, but is it any wonder that loneliness is considered a health epidemic?[1]

God created us for connection. "Two," Scripture says, "are better than one"—for all sorts of good reasons.[2] We need friends, individually and as a couple.

How do we get them?

Taking the Initiative

Thanks to Robbie's job with a company that had interests all over the country, we moved a lot when our children were growing up. Our daughter Annesley went to elementary school in four different states. People were generally welcoming when we hit a new community, but we got more than a few side-eyes. *How come you aren't really "from" anywhere? If you aren't with the military, what are you doing? Are you in witness protection?*

We never knew how long we'd be in one place, so I didn't waste time when it came to friendship forging. Church was always our main fishing hole, followed by the rec leagues where we met other parents on the sidelines. But I wasn't above picking folks out of the carpool lineup and asking if they wanted to get together. Which is how we wound up celebrating Robbie's thirtieth birthday, shortly after we moved to Atlanta, with twenty strangers— women I had met and invited to come to our house with their husbands and yell "Surprise!" when Robbie got home from work.

(He was surprised.)

I'm not suggesting you need to be *that* extreme in your friendship hunt, but I do want to encourage you to take the initiative. Look for couples with whom you have something in common, whether it's career paths, hobbies, or your children's ages. Because those birthday guests had been plucked from places like the church nursery drop-off and the preschool car line, they were in our same parenting season, and as our friendships grew, we became deeply invested in one another's children and protective of each other's marriages. And when we realized that most of us were sagging under the weight of what our friend Julie calls "Groundhog Day life" (wake up, kids to school, work, dinner, bed . . . and do it all over again tomorrow), and because it was February, we decided to spice things up with what we called a Midwinter Sizzle.

We asked another couple (whose ancestors had lived in Atlanta since before Scarlett and Rhett) to host the party with us. We charged the guests twenty-five dollars per couple to come, and at intervals throughout the night, we drew names from a hat to win romantic-themed prizes. At the end of the evening, when there was just one name left in the hat, we drew the grand prize—an overnight at the Ritz, complete with Sunday brunch. Childcare had been arranged beforehand, and couples came to the party with suitcases packed, so we all cheered for the lucky winners as they drove away. The only person to question the whole undertaking was our cohost's grandmother—a quintessentially Southern hostess—who liked the idea but was appalled that we would make our friends pay to come to a party.

Finding Acts 2:42 Friends

Sometimes it's not a geographic move but a new season that can leave us feeling isolated. Robbie and I hadn't gotten very far into our empty nest years when we realized that our social network was eroding. No longer did we have other parents to connect with in the bleachers at high school ball games, nor were we partnered with other moms and dads to help run important educational events like the Bazooka Blowout at the elementary school. We still loved spending time with our church friends, but even there we felt the drift as folks began spending weekends visiting their kids at college, babysitting their grandchildren, or enjoying their newfound freedom to travel.

One day, Robbie and I walked into a friend's home and saw Acts 2:42 painted on a breadboard in the kitchen: "They devoted themselves to the apostles' teaching and to fellowship, to the breaking of bread and to prayer." That's how Luke describes the early church, and when we saw the sign, we thought to ourselves: *That's it.* That's *the recipe for good friendship in every season.*

Honestly, though, that kind of friendship can be hard to cultivate. Where do we find companions who will be not just interested in, but *devoted* to, biblical teaching? To fellowship (Eugene Peterson's *The Message* says "life together"), shared meals, and prayer? We know plenty of folks who'd check one or two of these boxes (who doesn't love a good dinner party?), but all four?

Maybe you feel the same way. Maybe you know that a loving and supportive community is key to the long-term health of your marriage, and you're longing for an Acts 2:42 friend group, but your current social circle looks nothing like those early believers.

Maybe you're a woman who runs—literally or figuratively—with a group of gals who talk their way through the miles, complaining about their husbands and what they do (or don't do). Maybe you're a man who golfs with a regular foursome who tell stories and jokes they would never repeat to their wives. It may seem like lighthearted banter, but even the most casual conversations leave an aftertaste. "Words kill, words give life," Scripture says. "They're either poison or fruit—you choose."[3]

Take an honest look at the company you keep. If your friends don't prioritize marriage and speak well of their spouse, it may be harder for you to do the sometimes-hard work of strengthening your own relationship. Likewise, if your friends treat their marriage vows casually, you may be tempted to do the same. As Proverbs 13:20 says, "Breaking up is hard to do—unless everyone else is doing it."

(That's not really the way Proverbs 13:20 goes. The actual translation reads, "Walk with the wise and become wise, for a companion of fools suffers harm." The point is this: For better or for worse, we become like our friends.)

Surround yourself with people who have what you want in a marriage, who treat their spouse the way you and your spouse want to be treated. Ask God to give you—and make you—life-giving friends.

God has answered that prayer for us again and again. Once, shortly after we hit the empty nest years, we got a call from another gal whose youngest had just left for college. She and her husband wanted to cultivate some life-giving friendships of their own, and she was recruiting. Five couples from different parts of the country accepted her invitation to get together, and we've been meeting regularly now for more than a decade. We goof off like friends do, but we also lean in to each other's lives: *What are you doing to invest in your marriage? Where have you struggled at work? How might God want to use you and your gifts in this season? What are you doing to grow closer to him?*

> Surround yourself with people who have what you want in a marriage, who treat their spouse the way you and your spouse want to be treated.

The questions—and the answers—aren't always easy. When these friends challenge or correct us, it's out of love, but that doesn't mean the whole "iron sharpening iron" thing doesn't hurt.[4] Still, though, we are grateful. "Wounds from a friend can be trusted."[5]

As you pray about your own current and future friendships, keep the Acts 2:42 vision in mind. Be on the lookout for people with whom you can share Scripture, get caught up on life, eat (oh, you *have* to eat!), and pray. And when God answers your prayer and brings these people into your sphere, don't forget to extend grace. Just as there are no perfect marriages and no perfect parents, there is no perfect friend.

> *Just as there are no perfect marriages and no perfect parents, there is no perfect friend.*

There is no perfect friend—except the One who laid down his life for his friends.[6] As we cultivate our own friendships, we can ask the Holy Spirit to equip us to love like Jesus did, carrying one another's burdens, treating each other with love and humility, and being oh-so-quick to forgive.

Remember

Be good friends who love deeply. (Romans 12:10 MSG)

Reflect

Think about your circle of friends. Do you encourage and sharpen each other? Push one another closer to Christ? Support each other's marriages? Do you have friends who will pray for you and with you? Do you have fun with your friends?

Consider your own friendship style. Do you and your spouse rejoice over other people's victories, or do you struggle with jealousy? Do you consider your friends' needs and interests above your own? Think about the way Jesus loved and served his closest companions, and then ask the Holy Spirit to show you how to do friendship like that.

God created us for connection. If you long for deeper, more life-giving friendships, ask him to provide those—and be willing to take the initiative. Take a few moments to pray for your friends and then reach out to someone with an invitation. (It could be that God brought their names to your mind because they need friends as much as you do!)

Respond

Heavenly Father,

Surround us with friends who will encourage one another daily, so that none of us will be hardened by sin's deceitfulness. (Hebrews 3:13)

Bless us with friends who will sharpen us as iron sharpens iron and speak the truth to us in love. (Proverbs 27:17; Ephesians 4:15)

Give us friends we can come alongside in times of rejoicing as well as times of weeping. (Romans 12:15 KJV)

In our friendships, may we spur one another on toward love and good deeds. Prompt us to keep going to church and meeting with

other Christians so we can continue to encourage each other.
(Hebrews 10:24–25)

Help us identify and use our different gifts to live out your purposes, since we form one body in Christ and we belong to one another. (Romans 12:5–6)

Give us friends with whom we can be honest and vulnerable, confessing our sins without fear of judgment or rejection, and praying with one another. (James 5:16)

Provide mentors who will lead us, friends who will speak your word to us and model a life we want to imitate. (Hebrews 13:7)

Give us—and make us—friends who will love not just with words and speech but with actions and truth. (1 John 3:18)

Let us walk with the wise and become wise, since a companion of fools suffers harm. (Proverbs 13:20)

Make our hearts tender and compassionate as we enjoy the fellowship of good friends. Help us agree wholeheartedly with one another, love each other, and work together with one mind and purpose. (Philippians 2:1–2 NLT)

Surround us with a community of friends who can carry each other's burdens. (Galatians 6:2)

Let us be drawn to those who are devoted to godly teaching, to doing life together, to sharing meals, and to prayer. (Acts 2:42 MSG)

Loving through Suffering and Grief

A man sat down next to a grieving widow at her husband's funeral.
"Do you mind if I say a word?" he asked.
The widow nodded her head, and the man promptly stood up.
"Plethora," he said.
"Thank you," the widow sobbed. "That means a lot."

"Why do I have to keep praying? I am so very weary."

I could hear the discouragement in my young friend's voice. Her mother-in-law had been sick for two years, and doctors were holding out little hope. Not only that, but a recent restructuring in her husband's company had left him doing a job he did not enjoy, working under a boss he did not respect. It all felt, she said, like a lot. Like *too* much some days. Their marriage was strong, but the joy—the life— seemed to have evaporated.

I thought back to when Robbie and I were their age. We promised to love one another—for better, for worse, for richer, for poorer, in sickness and in health—but as we stood there in front of our family and friends, decked out in our beautiful wedding clothes and giddy with love, we had no idea what the future would hold. Career hurdles, financial setbacks, parenting challenges, my father's too-early death, and my own chronic health issues would all become part of our story, but we didn't know it. Not then anyway. Not on that glorious September day, smack-dab in the middle of hurricane season, with nary a cloud in the Virginia Beach sky.

Robbie and I knew what the Bible said about suffering —that God would be with us in our trials and that he promised to comfort us in our troubles—but those promises didn't seem relevant to our lives. We much preferred Psalm 84:11, the verse on our wedding program: "The LORD God is a sun and shield; the LORD bestows favor and honor; no good thing does he withhold from those whose walk is blameless."

Maybe every couple expects good things from God when they get married. Maybe nobody expects storms to come. Tiffany and Hunter certainly didn't, not with their baby's arrival just weeks away . . .

"The Hardest Thing"

Tiffany eyed her handiwork. Her son's bedroom was coming together nicely, the fresh coat of paint providing the perfect backdrop for his new "big boy" bed. *We'll move him next week*, she thought, giving her a whole month to pull the nursery together before his little brother (or sister?) arrived.

Suddenly, Tiffany felt a contraction. She'd been feeling full—bloated even—for a few days, but didn't every pregnant woman get uncomfortable near the end? Though Tiffany wasn't worried, to be on the safe side she decided to get things checked out. "You keep painting," she said, smiling at her husband. "You'll be finished before I get back from the hospital."

It would be a week before Tiffany came home, along with the devastating weight of a rare and life-threatening diagnosis—hydrops fetalis. At thirty-five weeks, her baby—a girl—was retaining fluid that was swelling inside her at an alarming rate. Tiffany's medical team was reluctant to induce early labor, preferring to buy time and hopefully to protect the baby's lungs, prescribing medicine and bed rest. Pushing back against the news of a 10 percent chance at survival, Tiffany and Hunter chose a name—Faith—and prayed for a miracle.

Soon, though, it became clear that Tiffany's own life was at risk, as the fluid built up in her abdomen. Hunter's fear for his unborn daughter was eclipsed by the very real possibility that his wife could die. "Save her," he prayed. "Please, Lord. I will do anything."

To Tiffany, life felt like a blur. After an emergency C-section, Faith was whisked away to a nearby children's hospital, with Hunter close behind. Never had Tiffany felt so alone. Fighting waves of nausea and pain, and with the blessing of her medical team, she managed to get to the children's hospital in time to see and touch her little girl—and to say goodbye.

It's okay, Tiffany sensed the Lord whisper. *I've got her.* As if to punctuate these words, a vibrant rainbow appeared outside the hospital window, just above Faith's tiny bed. Looking at the colors, Tiffany felt her heart tighten. "The hardest thing I've ever had to do," she says, "was to leave that hospital without our baby."

In the weeks that followed, life seemed to return to normal—for everyone except Tiffany. She scrolled through her social media posts in a haze, seeing her friends at concerts and out for dinner. Did they not know the anguish she carried? Even Hunter seemed to have buttoned up his emotions, throwing himself into work and putting their trauma behind him. "I'm just relieved we got through that," he said.

Tiffany knew she had not "gotten through" anything. Not knowing where else to turn, she immersed herself in the Bible, hoping to discover why her daughter had died or what bizarre lesson God might want her to learn. She desperately wanted another baby, but Hunter wasn't willing to try. "I don't want to go through that again," he said. "We have two children already—that's enough."

Tiffany couldn't believe how callous Hunter seemed. He refused to go to grief counseling with her, preferring to keep busy with work. Tiffany didn't think he was reading his Bible, and she wondered if he ever prayed. She recognized how judgmental she sounded, but didn't Hunter deserve it? Was he even walking with the Lord anymore? She didn't know. What she did know was that their marriage no longer had any emotional intimacy. Nor did they want to be together physically; in fact, they rented a small apartment so they could take turns giving each other space.

DINO. That word came unbidden to Tiffany's mind. "DINO" had been their marriage motto: Divorce Is Not an Option. *Maybe not,* Tiffany thought, *but I don't see any alternative.* "God, I know you can restore our marriage," she prayed, "but we can't. We've tried. If you want us to stay together, you need to change our hearts."

> "If you want us to stay together, you need to change our hearts."

As she had with the rainbow, Tiffany continued to see God in nature. Shooting stars, singing birds, even the wind whispering through the chimes outside her window all spoke to his presence. So did verses like Jeremiah 29:11, which brought reassurance that God had plans to give her hope and a future. Still, though, Tiffany didn't see how that promise could play out in real life, and she felt the tendrils of anger and bitterness begin to encircle her heart. Even her prayers took on a hard edge. *I don't know what you're doing*, she challenged the Lord. *But you'd better use all this pain for some sort of good.*

A year passed, and then another. Unable to say hard things to each other, Tiffany and Hunter journaled their thoughts, leaving the written words under their pillows for each other to find. That was something, Tiffany knew, but they needed more.

Hunter agreed. It had been three years since he and Tiffany had felt any connection or spark in their marriage. In fact, if he was being honest, he had to confess the relationship was over. Maybe not officially, but DINO or not, it was probably time. "I guess this is it," he said, over dinner one night.

"I guess so," Tiffany sighed. "It certainly has been a journey. I mean, I didn't even want to date anybody when we first met."

"I know," Hunter said with a smile, "but that didn't stop me from pursuing you."

Tiffany felt a tingle at the back of her neck. Something—she wasn't sure what—had changed in the atmosphere. And as they continued to talk about the early years of their love, it felt like something hard and icy was melting.

Hunter sensed it too. He reached for Tiffany's hand. "What are we thinking?" he said. "We don't want to end this . . . do we?"

Not trusting her voice, Tiffany just shook her head. No, she did not want their marriage to be over.

Looking back at that moment, Tiffany is convinced that God answered her prayer. He changed their hearts, taking the stone and making it flesh, doing what she and Hunter in their own strength could not do. And in the weeks that followed, they found themselves able to talk to each other—to grieve together—and romance blossomed. Their little apartment, once a place of escape and separation, became a secret love shack.

You Are Never Alone

Why did it take three years for God to answer Tiffany's prayer for her marriage? Why did they have to get to the brink of divorce before they could grieve together? Why did their little girl have to die?

Tiffany doesn't know the answers to questions like these. But the answers, she says, are not where her comfort comes from. It comes from knowing that God was with her in the midst of her pain, and that he is with her still.

Author Paul Tripp can identify with Tiffany's experience. Pointing to the two verses that have sustained him in suffering (Matthew 28:20 and Joshua 1:5, which promise the gift of God's presence), Tripp writes this:

> Our hope is not found in understanding why God brings hardship into our lives. Our hope is not found in the belief that somehow we will tough our way through. Our hope is not found in doctors, lawyers, pastors, family, or friends. Our hope is not found in our resilience or ingenuity ... Though we may look to all those for temporary help, ultimately our hope rests in the faithful and gracious presence of the Lord with us.[1]

Our hope is in the faithful and gracious presence of the Lord.

That theme—that our hope is in the nearness of God—runs throughout the Bible. God was with Joseph during the dark years when he was unjustly imprisoned. He was with Joshua when Moses passed the baton, leaving Joshua in charge of the Israelites. He was with David, keeping fear at bay in the darkest valley.[2] Every time anyone in the Bible came up against something hard, God gave them the promise of his presence to carry them through.

And he makes the same promise to us. He knows we will come up against hardship and suffering, pain and rejection,

> *Every time anyone in the Bible came up against something hard, God gave them the promise of his presence to carry them through. And he makes the same promise to us.*

questions that don't come with tidy answers. Through it all, he says, he will never forsake us, will quiet us with his love, and will be with us, to the very end of the age.[3]

Even as he offers the gift of his presence, God calls us to draw near. He calls us to pray, even in the face of weariness, discouragement, doubt, and pain. He tells us the same thing he told his disciples—that we should "always pray and not give up."[4]

Why? Why, to borrow a question from my young friend with the sick mother-in-law and the discouraged husband, do we have to keep praying?

We don't know—not exactly. But as we obey God—as we keep asking, seeking, and knocking—he promises that we will receive and will find, and the door will be opened.[5]

Will we get the answer we want? Maybe. Or maybe not. But as we press in, echoing Christ's "not what I will, but what you will" prayer in Gethsemane, transformation takes place.[6] No longer do we require a particular answer or outcome; instead, we have the freedom to grieve—to pour out our hearts to God, bringing him our disappointment, our questions, and our pain—knowing that his deepest desire is to comfort us and that he will satisfy us with his presence.

> We have the freedom to grieve—to pour out our hearts to God—knowing that his deepest desire is to comfort us and that he will satisfy us with his presence.

Robbie and I still love Psalm 84:11, but if we had to do our wedding program all over again, we wouldn't stop there. We'd add one more line—the last verse in the psalm—knowing that storms will come, but God's presence will be our anchor.

> For the LORD God is a sun and shield;
> > the LORD bestows favor and honor;
> no good thing does he withhold
> > from those whose walk is blameless.

> LORD Almighty,
> > blessed is the one who trusts in you.
> > > *Psalm 84:11–12*

Remember

> The LORD is close to the brokenhearted
> > and saves those who are crushed in spirit.
> > > (Psalm 34:18)

Reflect

It's understandable—and normal—to want to know the reason for suffering. Being in a difficult or pain-filled season rarely makes sense. And trying to figure out God doesn't help: "My thoughts," he says in Isaiah 55:8, "are not your thoughts." What does help, when you're in a place of suffering or grief, is knowing that God is in the pit with you.

Think back over the seasons of your marriage. Have there been times when you've sensed God's nearness in the dark? How have you experienced his help, his comfort, his power? Where do you need the gift of his presence today?

Whatever you've been through in your marriage, whatever you're up against right now, know this: God's thoughts about you are precious, and you are never alone. Read Psalm 139. Read it slowly, trusting—and praying—God's promises. He sees you. He will hold you. And his presence is with you always.

Respond

Heavenly Father,
We long to see your goodness in the land of the living. Help us be strong and take heart as we wait for you. (Psalm 27:13–14)

Be our God of hope. Fill us with all joy and peace as we trust you in this painful season, so that we may overflow with hope by the power of the Holy Spirit. (Romans 15:13)

Give us a crown of beauty instead of ashes, joy instead of mourning, and festive praise instead of despair. May our marriage become like a great oak tree, planted for your glory. (Isaiah 61:3 NLT)

Let us sense your nearness. Draw close to us and save us, for we are crushed in spirit. (Psalm 34:18)

How long, Lord, how long? Turn and deliver us from deep anguish; save us because of your unfailing love. (Psalm 6:3–4)

Comfort us in all our troubles so that we can comfort others. Make us alert to their needs and equip us to give them the same comfort you have given us. (2 Corinthians 1:3–4)

May we take refuge in you and be glad; let us sing for joy. Spread your protection over us and surround us with your favor, as with a shield. (Psalm 5:11–12)

Strengthen us so we do not lose heart. When we feel like we are wasting away, renew us day by day. Help us fix our eyes not on our temporary circumstances but on the unseen eternal glory that far outweighs them all. (2 Corinthians 4:16–18)

Help us trust you to do what only you can—raise the dead to life and with a word make something out of nothing. When everything looks hopeless, equip us to believe anyway, not on the basis of what we can't do, but on the basis of what you say you will do. (Romans 4:17 MSG)

Forgive our sins and heal our diseases. Redeem us from the pit. Crown us with love and compassion, and satisfy our desires with good things. (Psalm 103:3-5)

Let the redeemed of the Lord tell their story—the story of how you brought us out of darkness and deepest gloom. How you broke our chains. How you sent forth your word and brought healing. Let us give you thanks and tell of your works with songs of joy. (Psalm 107:2, 14, 20-22)

Be wonderful to us. Bring rains to our drought-stricken marriage. We have gone out with a heavy heart; bring us home laughing, with armloads of blessing. (Psalm 126:3-6 MSG)

Trusting God with Differences in Your Faith

First man: My wife says she wants me to be the spiritual head of our household and make all the major decisions.

Second man: How's that working out?

First man: So far, so good! We've been together for twenty-six years and there haven't been any major decisions!

"I knew I wanted to marry Janet the moment I saw her," Paul said. "We started dating, and I thought everything was going according to plan. But when I asked Janet's father for her hand in marriage, he wanted to know if I could be her spiritual leader."

The six of us—three couples—leaned in, drawing our chairs closer. New friends, we'd been sharing after-dinner stories about the early years of our dating and marriage, and Paul had captivated the group with his tales. I wondered where this one was going.

"I didn't know what a spiritual leader was," Paul continued. "It sounded like a Halloween costume. Did I need to get some kind of a hat? I wasn't sure. But I knew I loved Janet and I was going to do whatever it was that her daddy was talking about, so I said yes!"

Happily, Paul turned out to be a strong and godly husband, and he and Janet raised three children to know and follow the Lord. Over the years, Robbie and I have looked back and laughed as we thought about Paul and his "spiritual leader" costume. We sympathize with his bewilderment. The Bible doesn't actually use those words to describe a husband's role, and people who have not grown up with that language—or who may be unfamiliar with passages like Ephesians 5:21–33 (where God calls husbands and wives to mutual submission but places the headship role squarely on the husband's shoulders) —can be forgiven if they find such verbiage confusing.

We have three daughters, and whenever it looked like a suitor was approaching "legitimate" status (as in, someone who looked like he might be around for a while), Robbie invited him to have what came to be known as "The Talk." The conversations varied a bit, depending on each young man and his background or interests, but they all had one central theme. Robbie wanted to know where the fellow was spiritually and how he envisioned the relationship affecting our daughter. He knew that if one of our girls married someone who did not share her faith, either she would wind up hiding her passion for Christ (so as not to annoy or offend her beloved) or she would drift.

> *If one of our girls married someone who did not share her faith, either she would wind up hiding her passion for Christ (so as not to annoy or offend her beloved) or she would drift.*

As Robbie tells it, the nutshell version of The Talk went something like this: "You're a nice guy, and we wouldn't be having this conversation if my daughter didn't like you. She is precious to me, and you will treat her as precious. Your relationship will either draw my daughter closer to Jesus or farther away, and if I feel it is doing the latter, I will end it."

And then, Robbie says, if it was clear that the young man got the point, he would lighten things up. (Oh, how I would have loved to have been a fly on the wall for one of these interactions—and oh, how I adore our now-sons-in-law for hanging in there!)

"I Thought He'd Come Around"

Revie would have loved for her father to have given her husband The Talk before they got married. As it was, her parents emphasized their desire to see Revie marry "a good man," and they asked God to provide one. And when Peter showed up, it seemed God had answered their prayers. "He was smart and truthful and kind," Revie says. "The fact that he wasn't following Jesus didn't matter; I had no idea what it meant to be 'equally yoked.' To me, that meant you wanted two eggs, sunny-side up!"[1]

Looking back, Revie says she was counting on the power of love to work in her marriage. "Not God's love," she says, "but our love. I thought love was everything, and that since Peter loved me, he would want what I had. I thought he'd come around."

Not only did Peter not come around, but Revie's attempts to persuade him to consider Christ's claims seemed to backfire when after a short stint in church (a season during which Peter grew in his intellectual knowledge of God), he decided that the whole thing was "weird" and that he was, in fact, an atheist.

Revie was heartbroken. They had two children; what would Peter's rejection of Christ mean for their future? And what about love? Didn't that mean anything? Didn't *she* mean anything? The more Revie peppered her husband—"I tried shame. I tried manipulation. I told him he was hurting our family and missing out on the good life God wanted to give"— the more walls Peter put up. The more Revie felt her own heart growing cold. And the more isolated they felt from each other.

"Finally," she says, "I turned on God. I was sad, I was angry, and I didn't understand how he could give me a marriage that looked like ours looked—not when my church friends and I were praying so hard for Peter to come to his senses!"

Revie, she sensed the Lord say, *do you love me more than love?*

Revie felt her heart tighten. She knew what God was saying. She had made an idol out of "love," worshiping her ideal of what marriage should be, not who God was. As if confirming her thoughts, the words from Psalm 37:4 flashed in her mind: "Take delight in the LORD, and he will give you the desires of your heart."

Delight in me.

Slowly, Revie began to reorient her perspective, allowing love for the Lord to replace her love for love. That was the good news. The bad news was that Peter continued to wrap himself in darkness, distancing himself emotionally to the point where Revie wasn't sure she felt safe. "I will leave you!" Revie threatened. "Not if I leave you first!" came Peter's angry reply.

> She had made an idol out of "love," worshiping her ideal of what marriage should be, not who God was.

Deep down, Revie knew she wouldn't divorce her husband, and when Peter finally agreed to see a counselor in an effort to salvage their marriage, her relief was palpable. The counselor got right to the point. "Peter," he said, "you seem like a really smart man. If God was real, wouldn't you want to know him? Ask him. Say, 'God, if you are real, prove it.' If he is real, and if you are praying and seeking sincerely, he will show you. And if not, you'll be right."

Peter agreed to pray, and a few weeks later, he came to Revie. "I believe there is a God," he said. "I don't know about Jesus, or anything else, but I believe in God. Is that enough?"

Again, Revie sensed the Spirit's whisper. *"A smoldering wick he will not snuff out."* She recognized Isaiah 42:3 and knew she had her answer. "Yes," she said, "that's enough."

Revie watched and marveled as God slowly changed Peter's heart. "He was so hard," she says, "but from that small beginning, God gave him a heart of flesh—and today he's in love with Jesus. He is the husband I was always supposed to be with.

"But," she says, "I wasted a lot of years arguing and complaining. I wish, once God toppled the idols I'd put up about love and marriage, that I had just kept my mouth shut and prayed."

Winning without Words

While there are undoubtedly many men who pray for their wives' spiritual condition, the majority of people we hear from on this subject are women, and Revie is not alone in what she calls her "pushy" approach. Our friend Esther recalled how she kept score of the progress she and her husband each made in their faith—and how, in her eyes, he always fell short. He didn't want to pray with her. He was always more consumed with work than with their family, even when they went on vacation. He liked to relax with a bourbon (or two) at night; she didn't drink.

"I did everything I could think of to spark his interest in God," Esther said. "I gave him a personalized Bible with his name engraved on the cover, hoping he'd read it. I bought devotional books—one with a golfer on the front—hoping he'd pray. I gave him email contacts for Christian men we knew, wanting him to make them his friends."

Looking back, Esther realizes how silly all of this sounds, but it wasn't until her husband asked *her* a faith question that she came face-to-face with her own shortcomings. "Why do you think *your* relationship with God is better than mine?" he asked.

The Bible warns against allowing sin—including pride—to harden our hearts and deceive us.[2] It can be easy, especially for women, to fault our spouses when their spiritual lives don't look like ours. Trust me, I get it. I write books about prayer. I speak at Christian conferences. I use Bible verses as table decor at Thanksgiving, for goodness' sake. And while I've never purchased a devotional book with a golfer on the cover, now that I know they're out there, all the guys in our family might get one in their Christmas stocking.

These are the sorts of things that can look "Christian" to me. I'm not saying they're wrong . . . but are they what God really values? Might he be searching for something deeper?

"A holy person," writes Gary Thomas, "isn't known by what he or she doesn't watch, by avoiding a few forbidden words, or by attending a frequent number of religious meetings, but by how he or she treats fellow sinners."[3] Thomas goes on to say that if we really want to change the climate in our marriage, we should stop comparing our spiritual maturity with our spouse's and start comparing it with what God says about how we should love one another, as outlined in passages like Ephesians 4:2: "Be completely humble and gentle; be patient, bearing with one another in love."

No disrespect to the makers (or readers) of personalized engraved Bibles, but given the choice between that and a spouse who is humble and patient, I'd have to go with the latter if I'm trying to tap into life-shaping power.

The apostle Peter was nothing if not bold, but even he writes about sharing our faith with gentleness and respect.[4] And when it comes to marriage, his advice to wives with unbelieving husbands is that they should live their faith more than talk about it, so that even if the men do not believe, they will be "won over without words by the behavior of their wives."[5]

As we pray for our spouse's salvation and spiritual growth, let's also ask God to work in our hearts, helping us demonstrate the same loving-kindness and patience he shows toward us. It's his kindness, Scripture says, that leads us to repentance.[6]

Love, says 1 Corinthians 13:7, "always protects, always trusts, always hopes, always perseveres." Let's love one another not just for who we are now but for the people who, in God's tender hands, we are becoming.

> *As we pray for our spouse's salvation and spiritual growth, let's also ask God to work in our hearts, helping us demonstrate the same loving-kindness and patience he shows toward us.*

Remember

I will give them an undivided heart and put a new spirit in them; I will remove from them their heart of stone and give them a heart of flesh. Then they will follow my decrees and be careful to keep my laws. They will be my people, and I will be their God. (Ezekiel 11:19–20)

Reflect

If you are married to an unbeliever, or to someone who doesn't seem interested in moving closer to God, how has it impacted your relationship? How has it shaped your own faith? Do you find yourself fighting "the drift" or having to hide your enthusiasm for the Lord to keep the peace in your home?

When God tells us how to treat each other in marriage, no mention is made of spiritual "worthiness" as a condition for showing love and respect. Where do you need to confess things like spiritual impatience or pride? What can you do to show greater honor to your spouse, regardless of how they feel toward God?

God wants all people to be saved and to come to a knowledge of the truth.[7] Release your spouse into God's care, asking him to equip you to be completely humble, gentle, and patient as you trust him to fulfill his purpose in his perfect timing.

Respond

Heavenly Father,
No one can come to Christ unless the Father draws him. Draw _____, Lord. (John 6:44)

(For a wife) Make me willing to fit in with _____'s plans so that even if he refuses to listen when I talk about the Lord, he will be won by my respectful, pure behavior. Help me remember that my godly life will speak to my husband better than any words. (1 Peter 3:1–2 TLB)

(For a husband) Show me how to go all out in love for _____, exactly as Christ did for the church—a love marked by giving, not getting. Let me love my wife in a way that makes her whole, evokes her beauty, and brings out the best in her so she will be dressed in dazzling white silk, radiant with holiness. (Ephesians 5:25–27 MSG)

Work in _____'s mind and spirit, demolishing arguments and every pretension that sets itself up against the knowledge of God. (2 Corinthians 10:5)

Give _____ an undivided heart and put a new spirit in them. Remove _____'s heart of stone and replace it with one of flesh. Equip _____ to follow you and be careful to keep your laws so they will be one of your people, and you will be their God. (Ezekiel 11:19–20)

As I pray for my spouse's relationship with you, don't let me be anxious. Instead, fill my heart with thanksgiving as I present my requests to you. Let your peace, which transcends all understanding, guard my heart and my mind in Christ Jesus. (Philippians 4:6–7)

Let my light shine in our home so that _____ will see my good deeds and glorify you, Father. (Matthew 5:16)

It's your kindness that leads us to repentance, Lord. Help me reflect that same patience and kindness in our marriage. (Romans 2:4)

Open _____'s eyes. Turn my spouse from darkness to light, and from the power of Satan to God, so that they may receive forgiveness of sins and a place among those who are sanctified by faith in Christ. (Acts 26:18)

Thank you that you have plans to prosper us and not to harm us, plans to give us hope and a future. Prompt _____ to call on you and come and pray to you. Listen to them. Cause _____ to seek you wholeheartedly and find you. (Jeremiah 29:11–13)

Show me how to encourage my spouse daily so that our hearts will not be hardened by sin's deceitfulness. (Hebrews 3:13)

May we grow in the grace and knowledge of our Lord and Savior Jesus Christ. Be glorified in our marriage now and forever! (2 Peter 3:18)

Thriving in the Empty Nest Years

*After sixty-five years of marriage, my grandpa still calls
my grandma "honey," "sweetie," "baby," and "sugar."
I asked him for the secret to keeping love alive so long.
He said, "I forgot her name ten years
ago, and I'm afraid to ask."*

"People always say, 'The best is yet to come,' but it's not. Good things will come. But your best years—your most fun years—are behind you."

I searched my friend's face for any hint that she was joking, but she wasn't. Several years older than me, she had watched Robbie and me raise our children and she knew we were getting ready to send our youngest to college. She also knew I was feeling a bit melancholy about the transition, and I was surprised by her blunt assessment of the empty nest years.

That was then. This is now. And even though part of me acknowledges that my friend was right—I dearly miss the years when our nest was full, and even the subsequent "revolving door" season when our adult children pinballed in and out of our home—it's not an exaggeration to say that Robbie and I have settled into a new kind of "best." Not only is it a joy to discover a new normal with our kids (one where our main job isn't about teaching and correcting as much as it is about coming alongside them with love, prayer, and support), but we've found fresh delight in exploring life with each other.

> *Not only is it a joy to discover a new normal with our kids, but we've found fresh delight in exploring life with each other.*

(And not just because we can get a half-priced dinner without advance reservations at 5:30 p.m., which Robbie regards as a competitive win.)

We're enjoying this season of best because, for the first time in three decades, we are truly alone. Which means we have the time and the bandwidth to notice each other—to see and be seen. Which is kind of scary. And exhilarating. And not unlike when we were dating and would stay up half the night sharing our thoughts and dreams. Now we don't stay up half the night (not with those 5:30 dinners), but we do talk about "us" and the things our hearts hold, much more than we did when our calendars and conversations were crowded with kids.

Our friend Jim Burns understands this unexpected enjoyment. "Who would have thought that the most intimate times in a marriage aren't necessarily in the first few years but in the empty nest?" he writes. "In the second half, when you work at staying in love, the spark can continue, glow even brighter, and bring a warmth of intimacy that can happen only when you are willing to devote the time, energy, and attention not to settle for a mediocre relationship. You can be more united and experience more of an authentic oneness than you ever imagined."[1]

Jim is right—the spark *can* glow brighter, and second-half love can be incredibly rich and satisfying. But it may not seem that way right at first . . .

Even Exciting New Things Can Be Hard

Richard couldn't wait to get home after he and his wife dropped off their third son, their youngest, at college. Natalie had shed a few tears as she hugged him goodbye, but all in all, Richard thought, the move had gone smoothly. And on the drive home, when he hinted that they might want to try a skinny dip in the pool since they had the house all to themselves, Natalie gave him a sideways smile and reached for his hand.

They pulled into the driveway just after sunset. Natalie went upstairs to change while Richard grabbed a bottle of wine from the fridge. Wrapping a towel around his now-naked waist, he went out to the pool and turned the lights low.

Ten minutes later, he was still waiting.

"Nat?" Richard called as he went back indoors. Hearing no reply, he climbed the steps and heard a muffled sob coming from his son's room. There was his wife, splayed out on the bed facedown.

"I couldn't walk past his room," she wailed. "It's all just so . . . empty!"

Many parents can relate to Natalie's and Richard's experience: She feels like her purpose and identity have suddenly evaporated when the kids leave; he is excited to think he might get his girlfriend back. That's a generalization, of course; Robbie would tell you that he missed—and still misses—the noisy dinner table, the high school sidelines, even the "no man left behind" Sunday morning scramble as he tried to get the whole crew to church. And we both wondered what the future would look like for our marriage. Would we enjoy being together, just the two of us? Like, all the time?

It's not just a quiet house full of vacant bedrooms and empty chairs that can give rise to a mixed bag of emotions. We may struggle with regret as we look back on our parenting years; impatience, quick tempers, and unkind words can loom large in our memories. Or we may find ourselves unexpectedly lonely as our peers—the parents we sat with at ball games and worked with on committees at school—start to travel, go back to work, or spend more time with their grandkids. And if one or both of us are winding down a career, we may experience a whole new sense of upheaval as schedules and finances change.

"I married him for better or for worse," my friend Lucy laughed when her husband retired, "but not for lunch!"

> *We may struggle with regret as we look back on our parenting years. Or we may find ourselves unexpectedly lonely as our peers start to travel, go back to work, or spend more time with their grandkids.*

Christian authors and pastors like to point to Isaiah 43:19 as an anchor for hope during times of transition. "See, I am doing a new thing!" this verse proclaims. "Now it springs up; do you not perceive it? I am making a way in the wilderness and streams in the wasteland." That's a great verse—one you might put on a coffee mug or an empty nester T-shirt—but honestly? Even the most exciting "new thing" can be hard.

Finding Fullness in the Empty Nest

Author Susan Yates likens the empty nest years to Jell-O—"hard to grab hold of and constantly changing shape."[2] Part of the problem is that there is no "one size fits all" formula for navigating this season. There is, however, a handful of things we can do (and some things we should avoid) if we want love to flourish and grow as we adjust to our changing circumstances and roles.

Let's hit the don'ts first:

Don't expect your spouse or your job to fill the void left by your kids. It can be easy, especially for women, to feel emotionally bereft when the children leave, and we may look to our husbands for things like appreciation, affirmation, and understanding. For men, the temptation may be to pour themselves into their jobs. Instead of rushing to fill the hole with people or projects, talk with each other and be honest about how you're feeling. Figure out the next steps together.

Don't be quick to find fault. With more time to focus on one another, issues once masked by the cacophony of family living may surface. Some of these concerns may call for deeper conversations (like when one of you realizes that, with the kids gone, the other doesn't say much), and some will be ridiculously small (like the woman who told us she'd never realized "how loudly my husband chews" until they were alone at the table). Either way, big or small, every emerging question or concern will demand grace and a readiness, as Ephesians 4:2 puts it, to bear with one another in love.

Don't think that your relationship no longer matters to your kids. Just as your children watched how you treated one another when they were at home, they're observing—and learning from—how you invest in each other now. And with "gray divorce" on the rise (couples older than fifty who split up), the relational fallout is real—particularly for men, who are more likely (especially if they remarry) to find themselves alienated from their children. "Gray divorce can leave men cut off from crucial social support when they are most frail, and most in need of medical care, hospital visitors, and final reassurance of family love."[3]

As for what we *should* do, the list includes endless possibilities for enhancing communication, rekindling romance, and making the most of your new alone time together. Here are a few:

Do have fun. While this sounds simple or self-evident, just because you have more time once the children are launched doesn't mean you'll automatically have more fun. Make a list of ten things you'd like to do and then start doing them. Our friends Susan and Johnny went snowmobiling for the first time when they hit their seventies. Lynn and Ralph launched an annual couples getaway with a handful of newly minted empty nesters. Tim and Annabelle use the extra minutes they have in the morning to read the Bible out loud together—something they had never done when the children were home and mornings were a blur. Having fun doesn't always mean laughing out loud; anything that adds joy to your marriage can count in this column.

Do pray about your purpose. In addition to having more time, you have more wisdom and a better perspective than you had when you were younger. You have talents and experience to share and maybe more money to use. Make the most of the opportunities these resources afford by being intentional about where you invest them. Revisit some of the questions you likely considered earlier in your marriage—things like your strengths, abilities, and interests—and then be alert to the people or new ventures God brings your way.

> *You have talents and experience to share and maybe more money to use. Make the most of the opportunities these resources afford by being intentional about where you invest them.*

Do make your marriage a priority. You're never too old to keep stoking the fires of intimacy—romantically, emotionally, and spiritually. At one marriage conference Robbie and I helped facilitate, we met Gail and Gil, a couple who'd been married more than fifty years. "We keep dating each other," Gil said, "and we figure we're never too old to learn something new. Plus, when we made our vows on our wedding day, we weren't saying them just to each other; we were making a promise to God—and I'm not messing with that!"

All of these things—having fun, finding purpose, and prioritizing your spouse—are not unique to the empty nest years. But concentrating on them in a season when you're already in a transition of sorts can breathe fresh life into your relationship, whether your marriage needs a reboot or you just want to keep a good thing burning bright.

I mentioned in an earlier chapter how much Robbie and I love going to weddings and adding our hearty "We will!" when the officiant asks who will support the new couple. We also love weddings for a more personal reason. Each time a new bride and groom say their vows, Robbie takes my hand in his and we silently follow along. *To have and to hold from this day forward, for better, for worse, for richer, for poorer, in sickness and in health, to love and to cherish, until we are parted by death.*

Our older marriage conference friend was right. Wedding vows are promises worth keeping, to your spouse and to God, from the newlywed years to the empty nest years to forever.

Remember

The righteous will flourish like a palm tree . . .

They will still bear fruit in old age,

they will stay fresh and green.

(Psalm 92:12, 14)

Reflect

Think about your strengths individually and as a couple. Where have you seen growth happen over the years? What have you loved doing together? For what are you grateful to God?

Consider, too, the places where you may have unmet longings. Maybe you crave better communication, greater sexual intimacy, or spiritual closeness. Are there career plans, ministry goals, or family dreams you want to pursue? Give your spouse time to articulate their thoughts, and listen with grace.

Take a few moments to pray together or express support by sharing something you appreciate or admire about one another. Invite God to show you how he wants you to use your talents, money, and time in this new season. Be alert to any impressions you get—immediately and in the weeks ahead—and talk about these things with your spouse.

Respond

Heavenly Father,
May our marriage flourish as we mature. Equip us to bear fruit in our relationships and projects, even in old age, and may we always stay fresh and green. (Psalm 92:14)

Keep us sexually faithful to one another, rejoicing in each other as we did when we were younger, finding satisfaction in each other's embrace, and being intoxicated with love for each other. (Proverbs 5:18–19)

Make us alert to opportunities to tell the next generation the praiseworthy deeds of the Lord—your power and the wonders you have done. (Psalm 78:4)

Help us let go of our expectations about the empty nest season as we trust you to do immeasurably more than anything we could ask or imagine. (Ephesians 3:20)

Show us how to use the gifts we have received to serve others, as faithful stewards of your grace in its various forms. (1 Peter 4:10)

(For a wife) Help me to honor you by how I live. Equip me to teach others what a healthy marriage looks like, especially when it comes to training younger women how to love their husbands and children well. (Titus 2:3–4)

(For a husband) As an older man, may I exercise self-control as I navigate this season of life. Make me worthy of respect and help me to live wisely. Grant me a sound faith and fill me with love and patience. (Titus 2:2 NLT)

May we be like Joshua when he grew old, listening to you and accomplishing your purposes in the "land" you want us to possess. (Joshua 13:1)

Whatever we do in our empty nest years, may we put our hand to the plow without looking back, working with all our heart for you, Lord, not for people. (Luke 9:62; Colossians 3:23)

Give us eyes to see and a heart to perceive the new thing you are beginning to do. Thank you for being our waymaker and for bringing streams of water in a season that can feel empty and dry. (Isaiah 43:19 NIrV)

May we never ask, "Why were the old days better than these?" Instead, fill us with all joy and peace as we trust in you so that we will overflow with hope by the power of the Holy Spirit. (Ecclesiastes 7:10; Romans 15:13)

Thank you that we don't need a thing—we've got it all—and that you are right alongside us to keep us steady and on track in this spiritual adventure. You will never give up on us! (1 Corinthians 1:7–9 MSG)

Leaving a Legacy

Following a funeral service, the pallbearers carrying the casket accidentally bump into a wall. From inside the coffin they hear a faint moan. Opening the lid, they find the man inside alive! He jumps out, dances a jig, and lives another ten years before keeling over.

Once again, a ceremony is conducted. As the pallbearers pick up the casket to leave the church, the wife leaps to her feet and shouts, "Watch the wall!"

FINAL FAREWELL, *READER'S DIGEST*

"God is with you in everything you do."

That's what Abimelech, a Philistine king, said to Abraham when he broached the idea of a treaty, the first such recorded league in the Bible.[1] Abimelech was not a God follower, but he could see that Abraham was trustworthy and that God had blessed him. Abimelech wanted to be part of that legacy.

The Bible is full of similar stories, where onlookers—whether curious, skeptical, or eager—notice how God's people behave toward the Lord and each other. "Your very lives," Paul wrote to the Corinthian church, "are a letter that anyone can read by just looking at you. Christ himself wrote it—not with ink, but with God's living Spirit; not chiseled into stone, but carved into human lives—and we publish it."[2]

The same can be said of our marriages. How we walk through life together—for better, for worse—comes with the power to influence our communities, our churches, and our children, including future generations. "Your marriage is the message you are preaching to others," say authors Jennifer and Aaron Smith. "The way you and your spouse interact with each other reveals the gospel you believe."[3]

> *How we walk through life together comes with the power to influence our communities, our churches, and our children, including future generations.*

Our friends Lisa and Matt Jacobson, cohosts of *The Faithful Life* podcast, have eight children and a marriage that spans more than three decades, but based on how they treat one another, flight attendants and restaurant servers often mistake them for newlyweds. The Jacobsons don't choose their actions or words for the benefit of an audience, but they know people are watching and that their relationship, perhaps more than anything else, can demonstrate the power of God's love. "If the gospel hasn't made your marriage beautiful," Matt wonders, "then what are you inviting others to experience?"

Your Marriage as a Message

Robbie and I have seen the gospel's transformational power at work in our own marriage. Knowing both how sinful we are and how much God adores us is what prompts us to be patient and kind—not just with the preoccupied bank teller or the extra-slow grocery cashier, but with each other. It's what motivates us to love, even in the hard places. It's what equips us to forgive.

This power, of course, can shape every area of our lives, including our parenting, our careers, and our friendships. But as Robbie told one of the young men he mentors, "Getting marriage right—learning how to love and cherish your wife the way Christ loved the church—comes with a generational impact. Not only does the gospel impact you and your wife, but because your children will reflect your marriage, it will impact their children as well."

As you think about your own marriage, consider the message you want to send. Are you being kind to your spouse? Do you have fun together? Are you serving one another, as Galatians 5:13 puts it, "humbly in love"?

As Robbie and I answer questions like these, we are

grateful for the example of several older couples whose marriages have influenced ours. If you don't have any marriage mentors, consider asking God to provide some. Your relationship doesn't have to be formal. Some of the most powerful lessons Robbie and I have learned from our mentors have come from simply spending time together, enjoying a meal or a hike in the woods. We always feel free to ask questions— just as these couples feel free to challenge us with their own questions.

God knew we'd need mentors—and that we'd need to be mentors as well. The Bible repeatedly challenges us to encourage one another, to get wise counsel, and to imitate the faith of our leaders.[4] Paul wrote an entire letter to his protégé Titus to let him know how believers should live. Older women, he said, should be "reverent in the way they live," not slandering or drinking too much, but rather teaching younger women how to love their husbands and children. Older men should be "worthy of respect, self-controlled, and sound in faith, in love and in endurance" so they can encourage the young men to live the same way.[5]

The Bible repeatedly challenges us to encourage one another, to get wise counsel, and to imitate the faith of our leaders.

The best mentor, of course, is the Holy Spirit. It's his job, Jesus said, to teach us all things (which presumably includes how to do marriage well) and remind us of everything Jesus said.[6] As you consider the message you want your marriage to send, don't hesitate to enlist the Spirit's help. After all, as Galatians 5:22 reminds us, he is the one who produces genuine love in our hearts.

A People the Lord Has Blessed

Robbie and I count ourselves blessed to have parents who modeled what good marriages look like. Maybe you feel the same way. Maybe you've seen God's love in action in your family's life, both as you consider your parents and grandparents and as you look at God's faithfulness to your kids. Because of the legacy you inherited, you came into marriage knowing what it looks like to treat your spouse with kindness, to serve one another, to forgive.

Yet it could be that this hasn't been your experience, and you're reading this chapter—or this whole book—and feeling like you've missed out. Maybe you wish you had done a better job reflecting the gospel in your own marriage or that your parents and in-laws had given you a godly example to follow.

Maybe you think you'll never catch up.

Moses might understand how you feel. He knew all about missing out; he wasn't allowed to enter the promised land, even after leading the Israelites out of Egypt and then shepherding them for forty years in the wilderness.[7] Moses was well aware of the Israelites' past mistakes. But when it came to creating a legacy going forward, he was nothing if not expectant.

After chronicling Israel's wilderness history, Moses looked at the next generation—the group that had grown up in the desert because of their parents' unbelief—and said this:

> When the LORD your God brings you into the land he swore to your fathers, to Abraham, Isaac and Jacob, to give you—a land with large, flourishing cities you did not build, houses filled with all kinds of good things you did not provide, wells you did not dig, and vineyards and olive groves you did not plant—then when you eat and are satisfied, be careful that you do not forget the LORD, who brought you out of Egypt, out of the land of slavery.[8]

Did you catch that? Take a moment to go back and read it again. The young Israelites were about to enjoy every good blessing—flourishing cities, well-appointed houses, water and vineyards and bellies that would be oh so full—but *none of these things were their own handiwork*. Instead, they were evidence of God's provision, gifts he would provide instantly.

Like the Israelites' children, we all have a legacy—a spiritual inheritance, if you will—passed down to us through our families and through mentors, pastors, and friends. Some of us have a strong and godly heritage; others may be taking the first-ever step of faith in our family. We may come from very different places. Going forward, though, none of that matters—not where we have been, what our family has done, what our spiritual pedigree is, or how equipped we may feel. What matters is that God has a promised land he wants us to enter—a life in which our marriages glorify him and our prayers bear fruit.

> *God has a promised land he wants us to enter—a life in which our marriages glorify him and our prayers bear fruit.*

"As the Father has loved me," Jesus says, "so have I loved you. Now remain in my love."[9]

That's our legacy—a legacy of love. We are indeed more sinful than we could ever imagine and more loved than we could ever dream. The covenant promise fulfilled in Jesus is for us all.

> In my faithfulness I will reward my people
>> and make an everlasting covenant with them.
> Their descendants will be known among the nations
>> and their offspring among the peoples.
> All who see them will acknowledge
>> that they are a people the LORD has blessed.
>
> *Isaiah 61:8–9*

Remember

Rejoice always, pray continually, give thanks in all circumstances. (1 Thessalonians 5:16–18)

Reflect

Take some time to reflect on the story your marriage tells. What would you like to see God do with the rest of your life? What would you want him to change? If you were to list five key things you'd like to pass on to the next generation, what would they be?

Think of a couple whose marriage you admire. How have they walked through suffering or disappointment? How have they handled God's blessings? What have you learned from their example that you can apply to your own relationship?

Consider your own legacy. What are you grateful for? Where do you feel like you may have missed out? Commit your future—including generations yet to be born—to the Lord, knowing that you can pray with confidence and joy because "he who began a good work in you will bring it to completion."[10]

Respond

Heavenly Father,

May we continue to hope in you. Renew our strength. Equip us to run and not grow weary, to walk and not be faint. (Isaiah 40:31)

May we remain in you, and your words remain in us, so that we can ask whatever we want and it will be done for us—so you will be glorified and we will bear much fruit. (John 15:7-8)

Equip us to rejoice always, pray continually, and give thanks in all circumstances, for this is your will for us in Christ Jesus. (1 Thessalonians 5:16–18)

Don't let us hide your deeds from the next generation. Equip us to teach them about your powers and your wonders so that the next generation—even the children yet to be born—will know you, and in turn will tell their children so that they will put their trust in you and keep your commands. (Psalm 78:4–7)

May we trust in you with all our heart and lean not on our own understanding. Teach us to submit to you in all our ways, and make our paths straight. (Proverbs 3:5–6)

You have given us all kinds of good things. Don't let us forget you, but equip us to do what is right and good in your sight, so it may go well with us. (Deuteronomy 6:10–18)

Let us consider how we may spur others on toward love and good deeds. (Hebrews 10:24)

Teach us to number our days, that we may gain a heart of wisdom. (Psalm 90:12)

May we do everything readily and cheerfully—without bickering or second-guessing—so we can be a breath of fresh air in this polluted world. Let us give people a glimpse of good living and of the living God, carrying the light-giving Message into the night. (Philippians 2:14–16 MSG)

In everything, may we set an example by doing what is good. May our lives be marked by integrity and soundness of speech so that even those who oppose us won't have anything bad to say. (Titus 2:7–8)

May our marriage be marked by faith, goodness, knowledge, self-control, perseverance, godliness, mutual affection, and love. Increase these qualities in our lives so that we will be effective and productive in our knowledge of Jesus. (2 Peter 1:5–8)

Inspire us to keep your decrees and commands so that it may go well with us and our children after us and that we may live long in the land you have given us. (Deuteronomy 4:40)

May our marriage showcase the gospel as we submit ourselves to one another out of reverence for Christ, loving and respecting one another in a way that reflects the love between Christ and the church. (Ephesians 5:21, 32–33)

Let our light shine before others so that people will see our good deeds and glorify you, our Father in heaven. (Matthew 5:16)

Thirty-One Prayers for Your Spouse

"You're the answer to my prayers,"
the wife said to her husband. "You're not
what I asked for, but you are the answer."

Once upon a time, when our kids were mostly out of the nest and the odometer on my old Chevy Suburban crept toward the 200,000-mile mark, Robbie suggested it might be time for a smaller, more fuel-efficient car. Eager to demonstrate how well the newer, sleeker models worked, the salesman buckled himself into the passenger seat of one of his favorite models and started giving instructions. He had me punching the gas, taking on-ramps at top speed, and doing donuts in the dealership's parking lot. I was more than a little bit scared, but the car handled beautifully, and—much to my surprise—I felt safe, even on the sharpest curves.

It's like that, I think, with the Bible. God's promises are meant to bring safety and security to our lives. They are designed to keep us from spinning out when we hit a rough patch. They come with power to impart beauty. But until we take them for a test drive—until we start praying and believing the Scriptures on the real road of married life—we will never know how well they work.

It has been nearly forty years since Robbie and I stood in our newlywed kitchen, each of us secretly praying that God would "fix" the other. God told me back then that if I would stop nagging and start trusting, he would make Robbie into a husband who was better than anything I could have asked for or imagined. And he has—oh, how he has! And he has changed me as well.

And as we've tested God's promises over the years, he has also transformed how we pray.

No longer do Robbie and I ask God to change the other; instead, we pray for things like favor and blessing, protection and peace, wisdom and grace—God's bounty poured out on the other. Our marriage is far from perfect (and yes, I still nag sometimes), but as we've anchored our hope in

> *No longer do Robbie and I ask God to change the other; instead, we pray for things like favor and blessing, protection and peace, wisdom and grace—God's bounty poured out on the other.*

God's Word—trusting him to give us what Philippians 2:13 (NLT) calls "the desire and the power to do what pleases him"—we've been able to keep moving forward with confidence, even when the road is foggy or dark.

You've had the chance to test drive God's promises—to see how they handle—on all sorts of topics in this book. Obviously, though, there are places we have yet to explore. It can feel overwhelming sometimes. The good news is that it doesn't matter how many different needs or relationship hiccups we face; in all these things, God has us covered. There is no obstacle we will face in our marriages that he has not already anticipated and provided for in his Word. Whatever we need—physically, spiritually, or emotionally—God promises to supply it.[1]

> There is no obstacle we will face in our marriages that God has not already anticipated and provided for in his Word. Whatever we need, God promises to supply it.

Think about whatever it is that you're encountering, and ask God to show you how he wants to work in and through your marriage. As you read your Bible, be alert to the principles and promises you find, and use them to give shape to your prayers. "The Bible," writes Mark Batterson, "wasn't meant to be *read through*; the Bible was meant to be *prayed through*."[2]

Robbie and I have been reading—and praying—our way through the Bible for years, and we've lost count of how many times God has provided the exact word of encouragement, challenge, or wisdom we've needed for that particular moment or season. The margins of my Bible, as well as the lines in my journals, are filled with these well-loved verses and a record of how God fulfilled them.

We'll leave you with thirty-one of our favorite prayers, verses we return to again and again. Consider making your own list of prayers (feel free to adapt any of the ones in this book) and commit to praying for your spouse every day for a month. You don't have to pray long—a minute or two works, if that's all you can manage—but do pray sincerely, knowing that God's Word comes with power. It is alive and active, and it always accomplishes what he desires.[3]

And God is able to bless you abundantly, so that in all things at all times, having all that you need, you will abound in every good work.

2 CORINTHIANS 9:8

Thirty-One-Day
Prayer Challenge

If you'd like to access prayers like these in printable
form as a monthly marriage prayer calendar,
visit www.JodieBerndt.com.

Thirty-One Prayers for My Wife

Heavenly Father,

Fill _____ with all joy and peace as she trusts in you, so that
she may overflow with hope by the power of the Holy Spirit.
(Romans 15:13)

Don't let _____ worry about anything but pray about everything,
telling you her needs and thanking you for all you have done.
Guard her heart and mind with your peace. (Philippians 4:6–7 NLT)

May _____ enjoy good health and may all go well with her. (3 John 2)

Whatever _____ does, may she work at it with all her heart, as working for you, not for human masters, knowing she will receive an inheritance from you as a reward. (Colossians 3:23–24)

Don't let _____ fall short of your grace or have any bitter root grow up in her heart to cause trouble. (Hebrews 12:15)

Give _____ friends who will love not just with words but also with actions. (1 John 3:18)

May _____ act justly, love mercy, and walk humbly with you. (Micah 6:8)

Lead _____ beside quiet waters; refresh her soul. (Psalm 23:2–3)

Remind _____ that she is your masterpiece, created anew in Christ Jesus to do the good things he planned long ago. (Ephesians 2:10 NLT)

May _____ be completely humble, gentle, and patient, bearing with others in love and keeping the bond of peace. (Ephesians 4:2–3)

Prompt _____ to be quick to forgive others when they sin against her. (Matthew 6:14)

Make _____ quick to confess sin, secure in the knowledge that you will forgive her and purify her from all unrighteousness. (1 John 1:9)

Remind _____ that the tongue can bring death or life and that those who love to talk will reap the consequences. (Proverbs 18:21 NLT)

Make known to _____ the path of life; fill her with joy in your presence. (Psalm 16:11)

Equip _____ to be patient and kind, without any envy, boastfulness, or pride. (1 Corinthians 13:4)

Prompt _____ to call on you when she needs wisdom, knowing that you give it generously, without finding fault. (James 1:5)

Be faithful to _____. Strengthen and protect her from the evil one. (2 Thessalonians 3:3)

Remind _____ that you will meet all her needs according to your glorious riches in Christ Jesus. (Philippians 4:19)

May _____ commit whatever she does to you, confident that you will establish her plans. (Proverbs 16:3)

Give _____ the knowledge of your will and equip her to live a life worthy of you, God, pleasing you in every way, bearing fruit, and growing in her knowledge of you. (Colossians 1:9–10)

May _____ stand firm, always giving herself fully to your work, knowing her labor is not in vain. (1 Corinthians 15:58)

Let _____ delight in being a fountain of blessing in our marriage, satisfying me and intoxicating me with her love. (Proverbs 5:18–19)

Make _____ joyful in hope, patient in affliction, faithful in prayer. (Romans 12:12)

May _____ be sympathetic, loving to others, compassionate, and humble. (1 Peter 3:8)

Spread your protection over _____; surround her with your favor as with a shield. (Psalm 5:11–12)

As I cherish _____, may she exalt me; as I embrace her, prompt her to honor me. (Proverbs 4:8)

Cause _____ to love you with all her heart, all her soul, all her mind, and all her strength. (Mark 12:30)

Make _____ worthy of the calling you have on her life. Bring to fruition her every desire for goodness and every deed prompted by her faith. (2 Thessalonians 1:11)

Equip _____ to open her arms to the poor and extend her hands to the needy. (Proverbs 31:20)

May _____ be clothed with strength and dignity; let her laugh at the days to come. (Proverbs 31:25)

Turn your face toward _____ and give her peace. (Numbers 6:26)

Thirty-One Prayers for My Husband

Heavenly Father,

Equip _____ to be strong and courageous, not fearful or discouraged, and be with him wherever he goes. (Joshua 1:9)

Turn _____ from darkness to light, and from the power of Satan to you, so that he may receive forgiveness of sins and a place among those who are sanctified by faith. (Acts 26:18)

Help _____ be wise, making the most of every opportunity and knowing what your will is. (Ephesians 5:15–17)

May _____ serve you with wholehearted devotion and a willing mind; search his heart and understand his every desire and thought. (1 Chronicles 28:9)

Let your favor rest on _____. Establish the work of _____'s hands and make his efforts successful. (Psalm 90:17 NIV, NLT)

Equip _____ to be the head of our family and lead us well; may he love me and care for me as Christ does the church. (Ephesians 5:23, 29)

Whatever _____ does, may he work at it with all his heart, as working for you, not for human masters. (Colossians 3:23)

May _____ take delight in you; give him the desires of his heart. (Psalm 37:4)

May _____ walk in integrity and enjoy the security that brings. (Proverbs 10:9)

Don't let _____ be blown here and there by every wind of teaching or by the craftiness of people, but let him speak the truth in love and grow up healthy in you, robust in love. (Ephesians 4:14–15 NIV, MSG)

Keep _____ in perfect peace. Make his mind steadfast, trusting in you. (Isaiah 26:3)

When _____ is weary or discouraged, don't let him throw away his confidence. Instead, equip him to persevere in doing your will, knowing that he will be richly rewarded. (Hebrews 10:35–36)

Clothe _____ with compassion, kindness, humility, gentleness, and patience. (Colossians 3:12)

Make _____ quick to confess sin, knowing that you are faithful and forgiving and you will purify him from all unrighteousness. (1 John 1:9)

May _____ be always on guard, standing firm in the faith. Make him courageous and strong. (1 Corinthians 16:13)

Instruct _____ and teach him the way to go; counsel him and watch over him. (Psalm 32:8)

Protect _____ from lust, greed, and pride, which do not come from you but from the world. (1 John 2:16)

Give _____ the desire and ability to honor our marriage bed and keep it pure. (Hebrews 13:4)

Don't let _____ wear himself out to get rich or trust his own cleverness; remind him that he who gathers money little by little makes it grow. (Proverbs 23:4; 13:11)

Encourage _____'s heart; strengthen him in every good deed and word. (2 Thessalonians 2:17)

Give _____ friends who will sharpen him as iron sharpens iron and who will be sound advisers who can help him be victorious. (Proverbs 27:17; 11:14)

May _____ walk with the wise and become wise, for a companion of fools suffers harm. (Proverbs 13:20)

Pour out your Holy Spirit on _____. Fill him with love, joy, peace, patience, kindness, goodness, faithfulness, gentleness, and self-control. (Galatians 5:22–23 ESV)

Let _____'s love abound more and more in knowledge and depth of insight so he can discern what is best and be blameless and pure. (Philippians 1:9–10)

Keep _____ alert and of sober mind, since his enemy the devil prowls around like a roaring lion looking for someone to devour. (1 Peter 5:8)

Grant _____ aptitude for every kind of learning and work. Make him well informed, quick to understand, and qualified to serve in whatever job you have for him. (Daniel 1:4)

May _____ trust you as his good shepherd and enjoy the full and satisfying life you came to give. (John 10:10–11)

Let loyalty and kindness be written on _____'s heart so he will find favor and a good reputation with both you and other people. (Proverbs 3:3–4 NLT)

Pour out your Spirit on _____ and your blessing on his descendants. (Isaiah 44:3)

Work in _____ to will and to act in order to fulfill your good purpose in and through him. (Philippians 2:13)

Bless _____ and keep him; make your face shine on him. Turn your face toward _____ and give him peace. (Numbers 6:24–26)

A Note from Robbie

It never occurred to me when I graduated from the University of Virginia with an English degree that I would ever be involved in actually writing a book. I am more analytical than artsy, a trait I inherited from my accountant father, Bill Berndt. Calling my dad an accountant, however, is a label too narrow for the Renaissance man he is. Deep reader, thinker, friend to all, All-American athlete, gentleman farmer, a practicing accountant in his eighties—I am grateful to have had him as a mentor and friend and to be learning from him still.

Dad's finest accomplishment has been as husband to my saintly mother. Their love and relationship modeled the living of a scriptural marriage to my siblings and me. They love, cherish, submit, share mutual interests, and communicate in ways we all admire. My three siblings and I have made plenty of marriage mistakes, but we've all been married for more than three decades to our original spouses, thanks in no small part to lessons we learned from watching Mom and Dad navigate life.

When I met Jodie at a fraternity party in college at the age of nineteen, I knew she was special, and I have been focused on winning her heart since that moment. I don't deserve to be married to someone as beautiful, God-fearing, funny, and driven as my wife. God blessed me with her, and I thank him and strive to be a good husband (almost) every day.

Jodie has thick skin, which comes in handy when living with me. My analytical nature leads me to point out opportunities for "optimization" in everything I see. This trait has served me well in business and general decision making, but it leaves me a little callous when it comes to sharing with Jodie. I've learned how to answer questions like "Do these jeans make me look fat?" but in most areas of our married life I'm more focused on providing real answers than on catering to Jodie's emotions. I'm not interested in fixing symptoms of problems when the root issue needs to be addressed.

The writing of this book is no exception. Jodie wanted my input from the get-go, but as the chapters began to come together, she may have regretted asking. I reviewed every chapter, often batting the pages back to her with questions like "Is this deep enough? Have we addressed the real problem? Will a man appreciate or understand what we're talking about?"

At the end of the day, my involvement meant more work for my wife. But the end result is something we both think is accompanied by the power to draw us closer to Jesus, transform our relationships, and give us marriages that reflect what Paul calls the "profound mystery" of the gospel.[1] My hope is that by the blending of our thoughts in this book, we've shown love and depth in a way that speaks to both men and women. And I pray that your marriage will be strengthened and be a great source of joy and blessing in your life.

Acknowledgments

I wish I could remember the first person who encouraged me to begin praying for Robbie. Of course, I didn't know Robbie then (a manifestation of God's grace, given that my preteen self wore orthodontic headgear to school every day, topped with a pair of John Lennon glasses to highlight my affinity for the Beatles and compensate for my bookworm's nearsightedness). If I knew who had told me to start talking to God about my future husband—praying for his safety, his wisdom, his friendships, his faith—I wouldn't just thank them here, in the oft-overlooked acknowledgments pages; I would dedicate this whole book, and probably at least one of my children, to that person.

But since such knowledge escapes me, I will flash my now very straight teeth in a smile toward the host of mentors, colleagues, and lifelong friends whose love and expertise breathed vision and life into this book.

Carolyn McCready and Dirk Buursma, from concept

to completion, there could be no stronger (or kinder) editorial team. Your life-giving words produce fruit, à la Proverbs 18:21. And to Alicia Kasen and the "make-it-happen" Zondervan crew—especially Devin Duke, Kait Lamphere, Meaghan Minkus, Bridgette Brooks, Matt Bray, Paul Fisher, Curt Diepenhorst, Amanda Halash, and Abby Watson— thank you. What a joy it is to partner with such a faithful and creative team!

I'm grateful, too, to the couples whose stories appear in these pages. I know it's not easy to put your stuff "out there," even if you get to hide behind a fake name. Hebrews 6:10 comes to mind as I thank God for your candor and generosity, knowing he "will not forget your work and the love you have shown him as you have helped his people and continue to help them."

To our mentors and friends at Galilee Church (especially Dana and Andy, Anne Ferrell and Bob, Lisa and Tim, Lee and Bobby, Nancy and Steve, and Ruth and David—couples who have come alongside us to teach or host marriage-building events)—Robbie and I love watching God write your love stories. To our Empty Nest crew (especially Lynn, for recognizing the Proverbs 27:17 need to stay sharp), the Sisterhood girls (Alyssa B. for your humble heart and Kristin W. for the "kangaroo" vision), and my beloved "in the trenches" prayer partners who sent encouraging texts, cards, and even a plant (still alive!) during the long months of writing—thank you for getting it, and for keeping the golden bowls of Revelation 5:8 filled to the brim.

To my parents (Claire and Allen, and now Claire and John)—thank you for modeling what it looks like to cherish each other in all the better/worse, richer/poorer, sickness/health ways, and to have *fun* doing it. And to Robbie's folks, Mary Lou and Bill—thank you for welcoming me into your family and making it oh so easy to cleave. Your habitual love and selflessness set a high bar, but you make it look not only doable but also richly satisfying! #Goals!

To our children and their people—Hillary and Charlie, Annesley and Geoff, Virginia and Chris, Robbie and Mary—you've had a front-row seat to how the sausage is made, both in this book and in the bigger picture of our marriage. Thank you for being our biggest cheerleaders. May the Lord continue to make your love increase and overflow for each other and for everyone else, just as ours does for you (1 Thessalonians 3:12).

And, finally, to Robbie—my lover, my best friend, my most trusted advisor, my steady rock. You know I'm a music ignoramus, but I can't write this last part without wishing that the Spiral Starecase hadn't beaten me to it. Because I really do love you more today than yesterday . . . but not as much as tomorrow.

With all that I am and all that I have, I honor you.

Bible Translations

The following Bible translations have been quoted from in this book. The permission statements for the use of the various Bible versions have been provided by their respective publishers.

Notes

Introduction: Do What Works

1. Timothy Keller, *The Meaning of Marriage: Facing the Complexities of Commitment with the Wisdom of God* (New York: Dutton, 2011), 21.
2. Isaiah 55:11.
3. Proverbs 4:18 MSG.
4. See John 15:9–16.
5. Philippians 2:13 NLT.
6. Quoted in Elizabeth Bernstein, "The Science of Prayer," *Wall Street Journal*, May 17, 2020, www.wsj.com/articles/the-science-of-prayer-11589 720400.
7. Ann wrote these words in her foreword to my book *Praying the Scriptures for Your Life* (Grand Rapids: Zondervan, 2021), xiii.
8. The idea of showing support for your spouse (instead of praying together, if you're not yet comfortable doing that) came from The Marriage Course designed by the folks at Alpha. Get more info at www.alphausa.org.

Chapter 1: Getting Started

1. Isaiah 7:11 MSG.
2. Stanley Hauerwas, quoted in Timothy Keller, *The Meaning of Marriage: Facing the Complexities of Commitment with the Wisdom of God* (New York: Dutton, 2011), 38.
3. Quoted in Dale Anderson, "Reporters' Notebook: Jan. 31, 2022—Trying the Knot," *Buffalo News*, January 31, 2022, www.buffalonews.com/news /local/reporters-notebook-jan-31-2022-trying-the-knot/article_1ed56a0e -8179-11ec-955e-938d65ed9151.html.

4. See Maggie Gallagher, "Why Marriage Is Good for You," *City Journal*, Autumn 2000, www.city-journal.org/html/why-marriage-good-you -12002.html.
5. John 15:7.
6. Psalm 116:2 NLT; Isaiah 55:11.

Chapter 2: Fulfilling Your Purpose

1. *The Book of Common Prayer* (New York: Seabury, 1977), 423.
2. Genesis 1:28.
3. See Genesis 1:27–28; John 2:1–11; Ephesians 5:21–33.
4. See Genesis 9:7; 17:6; 41:52; Psalm 1:1–3; John 15:16.
5. To read more about the Bethkes' pillars or for help creating your own vision statement, please visit www.familyteams.com.
6. Stephen R. Covey, *The Seven Habits of Highly Effective People* (New York: Fireside, 1990), 108–9.
7. John 15:5.
8. John 15:7–8.
9. Job 42:2.
10. The link between relationship satisfaction and prayer is detailed in a study by Christopher G. Ellison, Amy M. Burdette, and W. Bradford Wilcox titled "The Couple That Prays Together: Race and Ethnicity, Religion, and Relationship Quality among Working-Age Adults." *Journal of Marriage and Family* 72, no. 4 (2010): 963–75, www.jstor.org/stable /40864957. This connection is also cited by Jim and Cathy Burns in their book *Closer: 52 Devotions to Draw Couples Together* (Bloomington, MN: Bethany House, 2009), 141–42.
11. See Ephesians 2:10.
12. James Strong, *Strong's Exhaustive Concordance of the Bible* (Peabody, MA: Hendrickson, 2007), 1489.
13. See Psalm 1:1–3.

Chapter 3: Leaving and Cleaving

1. Nicky Gumbel, "How to Stay on Track," The Bible in One Year, https:// bibleinoneyear.org/en/classic/27.
2. Genesis 2:24.
3. See Genesis 29; 38; 1 Samuel 25:44.
4. See Matthew 1:1–16.
5. See the book of Ruth; Matthew 1:1–17; Luke 4:38–39; Exodus 18:1–27.

6. Deuteronomy 5:16.
7. For more on the love languages and how they work, check out Gary Chapman, *The Five Love Languages: The Secret to Love That Lasts*, rev. ed. (Chicago: Northfield, 2015).
8. See Colossians 1:16–17.

Chapter 4: Growing in Kindness

1. 1 Corinthians 13:4.
2. Romans 2:4.
3. For this quote and other excerpts from the Gottmans' research cited in this chapter, see Emily Esfahani Smith, "Masters of Love," *Atlantic*, June 12, 2014, www.theatlantic.com/health/archive/2014/06/happily -ever-after/372573.
4. See Tara Parker-Pope, "The Generous Marriage," *New York Times*, Well, December 8, 2011, https://well.blogs.nytimes.com/2011/12/08/is -generosity-better-than-sex.
5. Beth Moore, *Esther: It's Tough Being a Woman* (Nashville: Lifeway, 2008), 65.
6. Romans 7:18.
7. Ezekiel 36:26–27.
8. Galatians 5:22–23 ESV.
9. Jeannie Cunnion, *Don't Miss Out: Daring to Believe Life Is Better with the Holy Spirit* (Bloomington, MN: Bethany House, 2021), 168.

Chapter 5: Talking with Love

1. See Joel and Nina Schmidgall, *Praying Circles around Your Marriage* (Grand Rapids: Zondervan, 2019), 77.
2. See Drs. Les and Leslie Parrott, "Become Your Spouse's Publicist," Focus on the Family, January 17, 2017, www.focusonthefamily.com/marriage /become-your-spouses-publicist.
3. For information about this course, please visit www.themarriagecourse.org.
4. Nicky and Sila Lee, *The Marriage Book: How to Build a Lasting Relationship* (Deerfield, IL: Alpha, 2000), 50.
5. See John 5:6; Matthew 8:26; 21:28.
6. See John 21:15–17.

Chapter 6: Learning to Listen

1. James 1:19.

2. Gary Chapman, *The Five Love Languages: The Secret to Love That Lasts* (Chicago: Northfield, 2010), 62–63.

3. Stephen R. Covey, *The Seven Habits of Highly Effective People* (New York: Fireside, 1990), 239.

4. See "Attention Spans," Consumer Insights Microsoft Canada (Spring 2015), 6, https://dl.motamem.org/microsoft-attention-spans-research -report.pdf; Nicky and Sila Lee, *The Marriage Book: How to Build a Lasting Relationship* (Deerfield, IL: Alpha, 2000), 62.

5. See Lee, *Marriage Book*, 63–64.

6. Luke 18:27.

7. See, for instance, Job 33:16 ESV; Proverbs 20:12.

8. Lisa Jacobson and Phylicia Masonheimer, *The Flirtation Experiment: Putting Magic, Mystery, and Spark into Your Everyday Marriage* (Nashville: W Publishing, 2021), 102.

9. James 1:23–24.

10. Psalm 116:2 NLT.

Chapter 7: Protecting Your Marriage

1. John Van Epp and J. P. De Gance, "Most Churches Lack a 'Marriage 911': Here's Why That Needs to Change," Institute for Family Studies, November 4, 2021, https://ifstudies.org/blog/most-churches-lack-a -marriage-911-heres-why-that-needs-to-change.

2. Genesis 4:7; 1 Peter 5:8.

3. Joel and Nina Schmidgall, *Praying Circles around Your Marriage* (Grand Rapids: Zondervan, 2019), 122.

4. This prayer is an adaptation of Psalm 51, which reflects King David's prayer after he had committed adultery with Bathsheba.

5. Romans 12:3 NLT.

Chapter 8: Handling Conflict

1. Charles Spurgeon, "No. 2974: A Wafer of Honey: A Sermon Published on Thursday, February 8th, 1906," Spurgeon Center, www.spurgeon .org/resource-library/sermons/a-wafer-of-honey/#flipbook, accessed September 10, 2022.

2. James 1:2–4.

3. Cited in John Gottman, *The Truth about Expectations in Relationships*, Gottman Institute, www.gottman.com/blog/truth-expectations -relationships, accessed September 10, 2022.

4. John 10:10.
5. Ephesians 5:15–17 NLT.
6. See Daily Mail Reporter, "Couples Argue 312 Times a Year (Mostly on Thursday at 8pm for Ten Minutes)," *Daily Mail*, January 18, 2011, www.dailymail.co.uk/femail/article-1348308/Couples-argue-312-year-likely-8pm-10-minutes.html.
7. Shaunti Feldhahn, *The Good News about Marriage: Debunking Discouraging Myths about Marriage and Divorce* (Colorado Springs: Multnomah, 2014), 3–4.
8. Ephesians 4:26–27.
9. Quoted in Emily Esfahani Smith, "Masters of Love," *Atlantic*, June 12, 2014, www.theatlantic.com/health/archive/2014/06/happily-ever-after/372573.
10. C. Munsey, "Prayer Takes the Edge Off, a New Study Suggests," *Monitor on Psychology* 42, no. 6 (June 2011): 10, www.apa.org/monitor/2011/06/prayer.
11. For more on loving people, see Day 4 in my book *Praying the Scriptures for Your Life: 31 Days of Abiding in the Presence, Provision, and Power of God* (Grand Rapids: Zondervan, 2021), 54–57.

Chapter 9: Experiencing Forgiveness

1. Gary Thomas, *Cherish: The One Word That Changes Everything for Your Marriage* (Grand Rapids: Zondervan, 2017), 154.
2. C. S. Lewis, *The Weight of Glory* (1949; repr., New York: HarperOne, 2001), 182.
3. Quoted in "Remembering Ruth Bell Graham," Billy Graham Library, July 1, 2013, https://billygrahamlibrary.org/remembering-ruth-bell-graham-2.
4. Timothy Keller, *The Meaning of Marriage: Facing the Complexities of Commitment with the Wisdom of God* (New York: Dutton, 2011), 109, italics in original.
5. God's love in the face of our unfaithfulness is a theme that runs throughout Scripture; see Hosea 2 for one especially vivid example.
6. To find a Christian counselor in your area, contact Focus on the Family (www.focusonthefamily.com/get-help) or the American Association of Christian Counselors (www.aacc.net).
7. Lewis B. Smedes, *Forgive and Forget: Healing the Hurts We Don't Deserve* (San Francisco: HarperSanFrancisco, 1984), 133.
8. See Philippians 2:13 NLT; Romans 8:26; James 4:6 ESV.

9. 1 John 1:9.

10. 1 John 4:19.

11. Keller, *Meaning of Marriage*, 48.

Chapter 10: Enjoying Good Sex

1. *Everybody Loves Raymond*, season 6, episode 2, "No Roll!" written by Aaron Shure, aired October 1, 2001.

2. Cited in Debra Fileta, *Choosing Marriage: Why It Has to Start with We > Me* (Eugene, OR: Harvest House, 2018), 159.

3. User Reviews: Featured Review, *"Everybody Loves Raymond*: 'No Roll!'" IMDb, www.imdb.com/title/tt0763255, accessed September 10, 2022.

4. Gary Thomas and Debra Fileta, *Married Sex: A Christian Couple's Guide to Reimagining Your Love Life* (Grand Rapids: Zondervan, 2021), 19. Fileta, a licensed counselor, teamed up with relationship expert Gary Thomas to write this practical, biblical, and (to me, Jodie) blushworthy book—and one that is absolutely worth reading if this is an area where you've struggled to connect with your spouse (or if you just want to follow Ray Romano's lead and upgrade your sex life).

5. See Proverbs 5:18–19; Song of Songs 7:11–12; 1 Corinthians 7:5.

6. To find a good counselor, contact the American Association of Christian Counselors (www.aacc.net) or Focus on the Family (www.focusonthe family.com/get-help).

7. Romans 9:32 MSG.

8. Thomas and Fileta, *Married Sex*, 88.

9. See Gary and Barbara Rosberg, *The Five Sex Needs of Men and Women: Discover the Secrets to Great Sex in a Godly Marriage* (Carol Stream, IL: Tyndale, 2006), 40.

10. Thomas and Fileta, *Married Sex*, 74, italics in original.

11. See Proverbs 2:17.

12. See Genesis 2:25.

Chapter 11: Handling Money

1. See Brandon Park, "2,350 Bible Verses on Money," ChurchLeaders, November 30, 2017, https://churchleaders.com/outreach-missions /outreach-missions-articles/314227-2350-bible-verses-money.html.

2. See, for example, 1 Chronicles 29:14; Job 41:11.

3. Luke 16:13.

4. Matthew 5:16.

5. Some of the illustrations are outdated, but you can read more about the purpose of money and other time-tested financial planning principles in Ron and Judy Blue with Jodie Berndt, *Money Talks and So Can We* (Grand Rapids: Zondervan, 1999).
6. Debt really can be a crippling burden. If you need help getting out from under the pile or just making a spending plan you can live with, check out the resources available at www.ramseysolutions.com.
7. See, for example, Psalm 24:1.
8. Philippians 4:19.
9. Matthew 6:8.
10. 1 Corinthians 1:10; Philippians 2:2–3.
11. See Romans 8:28.
12. See 2 Corinthians 9:8–11.

Chapter 12: Serving Each Other in Love

1. Titus 3:1; 1 Peter 4:10; Galatians 5:13.
2. Lisa writes about her one-hundred-day Love Challenge in her book *One Hundred Ways to Love Your Husband: The Simple, Powerful Path to a Loving Marriage* (Grand Rapids: Revell, 2019), 68.
3. Timothy Keller, *The Meaning of Marriage: Facing the Complexities of Commitment with the Wisdom of God* (New York: Dutton, 2011), 57.
4. Galatians 6:7–9.
5. Matthew 20:28.
6. Ephesians 5:21.
7. Ephesians 5:18.
8. These traits and the other fruit of the Spirit are listed in Galatians 5:22–23 (ESV).
9. Philippians 2:5.
10. Gary Thomas, *Cherish: The One Word That Changes Everything for Your Marriage* (Grand Rapids: Zondervan, 2017), 17.
11. Ann Voskamp, *Waymaker: Finding the Way to the Life You've Always Dreamed Of* (Nashville: W Publishing, 2022), 71.

Chapter 13: Having Fun Together

1. Mayo Clinic Staff, "Stress Relief from Laughter? It's No Joke," *Healthy Lifestyle*, July 29, 2021, www.mayoclinic.org/healthy-lifestyle/stress-management/in-depth/stress-relief/art-20044456.
2. Mayo Clinic Staff, "Stress Relief from Laughter?"

3. "The Celebration and Blessing of a Marriage," in *The Book of Common Prayer* (New York: Seabury, 1977), 423.

4. Jodie Berndt, *Praying the Scriptures for Your Teens: Opening the Door for God's Provision in Their Lives*, rev. ed. (Grand Rapids: Zondervan, 2021), 2.

5. Jim Burns, *Have Serious Fun: And 12 Other Principles to Make Each Day Count* (Grand Rapids: Zondervan, 2021), 9–10.

6. Psalm 16:11.

7. Jeremy and Audrey Roloff, *Creative Love: 10 Ways to Build a Fun and Lasting Love* (Grand Rapids: Zondervan, 2021), 31.

8. Lisa Jacobson and Phylicia Masonheimer, *The Flirtation Experiment: Putting Magic, Mystery, and Spark into Your Everyday Marriage* (Nashville: W Publishing, 2021), 41.

9. See, for example, John 15:11 NLT; Psalm 126:2.

10. John 15:11 ESV.

Chapter 14: Parenting Priorities

1. Quoted in *City Slickers*, directed by Ron Underwood, screenplay by Lowell Ganz and Babaloo Mandel (Culver City, CA: Columbia Pictures, 1991).

2. Rachel Gillett, "11 Ways Your Marriage Could Be Affecting Your Kids' Success," *Business Insider*, August 31, 2016, www.businessinsider.com /how-your-marriage-influences-your-childs-success-2016-8.

3. See Gillett, "11 Ways."

4. Psalm 78:4, 6–7.

Chapter 15: Making Good Friends

1. See Madeline Dangerfield-Cha and Joy Zhang, "Solving the Loneliness Epidemic, Two Generations at a Time," *Stanford Social Innovation Review*, March 29, 2021, https://doi.org/10.48558/Q5N3-0503.

2. Ecclesiastes 4:9.

3. Proverbs 18:21 MSG.

4. See Proverbs 27:17.

5. Proverbs 27:6.

6. See John 15:13.

Chapter 16: Loving through Suffering and Grief

1. Paul David Tripp, "Two Verses Held Me through Suffering," Desiring God, April 11, 2019, www.desiringgod.org/articles/two-verses-held-me -through-suffering.

2. See Genesis 39:21; Deuteronomy 31:6; Psalm 23:4.
3. Hebrews 13:5; Zephaniah 3:17 ESV; Matthew 28:20.
4. Luke 18:1.
5. See Matthew 7:7–8.
6. Mark 14:36.

Chapter 17: Trusting God with Differences in Your Faith

1. The reference to being "yoked" comes from 2 Corinthians 6:14, where Paul warns the Corinthians not to be "yoked together" with unbelievers.
2. See, for example, Obadiah 3; Hebrews 3:12–13.
3. Gary Thomas, *Cherish: The One Word That Changes Everything for Your Marriage* (Grand Rapids: Zondervan, 2017), 154–55.
4. See 1 Peter 3:15.
5. 1 Peter 3:1.
6. See Romans 2:4.
7. See 1 Timothy 2:4.

Chapter 18: Thriving in the Empty Nest Years

1. Jim Burns, *Finding Joy in the Empty Nest: Discover Purpose and Passion in the Next Phase of Life* (Grand Rapids: Zondervan, 2022), 75.
2. Barbara Rainey and Susan Yates, *Barbara and Susan's Guide to the Empty Nest: Discovering New Purpose, Passion, and Your Next Great Adventure* (Little Rock, AR: FamilyLife, 2008), 9.
3. Kay Hymowitz, "The Aftermath of Gray Divorce for Men, Women, and Their Adult Children," Institute for Family Studies, October 25, 2021, https://ifstudies.org/blog/the-aftermath-of-gray-divorce-for-men-women -and-their-adult-children.

Chapter 19: Leaving a Legacy

1. See Genesis 21:22–34.
2. 2 Corinthians 3:1–3 MSG.
3. Aaron and Jennifer Smith, *Marriage after God: Chasing Boldly after God's Purpose for Your Life Together* (Grand Rapids: Zondervan, 2019), 94.
4. See, for example, 1 Thessalonians 5:11; Proverbs 1:5; Hebrews 13:7.
5. Titus 2:1–8.
6. See John 14:26.
7. See Deuteronomy 32:50–52.
8. Deuteronomy 6:10–12.

9. John 15:9.

10. Philippians 1:6 ESV.

Chapter 20: Thirty-One Prayers for Your Spouse

1. See Philippians 4:19.

2. Mark Batterson, *The Circle Maker: Praying Circles around Your Biggest Dreams and Greatest Fears* (Grand Rapids: Zondervan, 2011), 96, italics in original.

3. See Hebrews 4:12; Isaiah 55:11.

Afterword: A Note from Robbie

1. Ephesians 5:32.